DYING IS WEIRD

A Journey of Enlightenment

Kathleen Westberg

Dying is Weird

A Journey of Enlightenment

Kathleen Westberg

Published by 1st World Publishing
P.O. Box 2211, Fairfield, Iowa 52556
tel: 641-209-5000 • fax: 866-440-5234
web: www.1stworldpublishing.com

First Edition

LCCN: 2015932997

ISBN: 978-1-4218-8699-2

Eskimo Legend says the Aurora Borealis are the torches in the hands of our Ancestor Spirits, lighting the way for the souls of those who have just died, to lead them to the hereafter, a place where illness and pain are no more.

This book is dedicated to those souls

Acknowledgements

I have to start by thanking my daughter Lora, who insisted on my revisiting all my past experiences to get to the depth of all my emotions.

Gina, my granddaughter, for saying "Gram, lets wrap this story up and see where it goes," and continued to be my sounding board until my story seemed right.

And to my granddaughter Tina, my computer whiz, who was always on standby for questions and problems—and there were many.

My wonderful husband, family, and many friends, who were a part of my journey and whose encouragement spurred me on. You are my joy.

A special thanks to Dawn and Jodie who helped pull off a happenstance meeting with Vernon Sylvest; he read my story, gave me great feedback, and pointed me in the right direction for getting it published.

And finally, to Nandini and Rodney Charles at 1st World Publishing, for the kindness they have shown me.

Foreword

Novelist Mona Simpson wrote a lyrically beautiful eulogy in the New York Times for her half-brother Steve Jobs, in which she tried to distill the essence of what she had observed and learned from her famous tech-mogul sibling. Mona was raised by a single mother and had grown up separately from Jobs, who her mother had given up for adoption years before Mona was born. But Steve and Mona rapidly became friends after they first found out about each other in 1985. They developed a special closeness, and Steve shared many personal aspects of his life with his newfound sister as their appreciation for each other grew over the years. As Steve's death became inevitable, Mona and Steve's family rallied around him as they tried to comfort each other and prepare for the moment of transition.

Mona described how Steve's breathing changed in his final hours, becoming more conscious and deliberate – even as he was becoming weaker. She wrote, "Death didn't happen to Steve, he achieved it… His breath reflected "an arduous journey, some steep path, altitude." And in his final moments on this Earth, Steve looked for a long time at his loved ones gathered there, and then over their shoulders, and his last words were, "OH WOW. OH WOW. OH WOW." A journalist friend of mine mused that alongside Steve Jobs' many entrepreneurial and technological accomplishments, these final words were a revelation of spiritual beauty that should also be considered part of his legacy, his contributions to broadening our humanity.

We are all captive to death – to transitions in and out of this world, and we are forever trying to understand what mysteries lie beyond the veil. This is what makes Kathleen Westberg's Dying is Weird: A Journey of Enlightenment such a compelling, humble and beautifully authentic book. Kathleen's life story and her encounters with death take us to the edge of this veil where we can sense some of the truth and wonder and mystery of what connects us to the afterlife and the feeling that our loved ones are still with us, beyond the limits of physical perception. Kathleen's journey is a journey through time, generations, unseen dimensions and unfamiliar learning that defies our social expectations and comfort zones in refreshing ways.

Dying is Weird: A Journey of Enlightenment is a tapestry of varied features that represents many things; a family and its turn of the century Catholic immigrant roots, the life spans of mother-daughter and father-daughter relationships, a story of growing up in the stoic atmosphere of rural Wisconsin, America's Heartland; a story about encountering death at an early age and a continual search for answers. In loving and often humorous conversational voice, Kathleen introduces us to her grandparents, her mother and father, her brothers, sisters and cousins and the tenderhearted feelings that are evoked as their lives unfold and at times she has to face their death. But these experiences awaken a quest for meaning and answers, leading this down-to-earth Midwestern woman to find books, classes, mentors and doorways into unfamiliar concepts like clairvoyance, astral projection, reincarnation, the Akashic records, massage, healing touch and meditation. Despite resistance from her family and friends, Kathleen feels drawn to explore worlds that test her understanding and beliefs, and in the process, her life is enriched immeasurably.

Kathleen experiences premonitions, has visits from her dead mother and brother, assists her father in his transition and also experiences his presence after he dies. As she grows in her awareness and understanding, Kathleen also touches the hearts of her family and the staff and patients in the medical clinic where she works.

Kathleen's book has an extraordinary impact in the disguise of seemingly ordinary relationships and events of time. It brings to mind a quote from Dr. Wayne Dyer:

"Remind yourself that God created you in perfect love that is changeless and eternal. Your body is changing, as is your mind, so you are not that body or that mind. You were created as a spirit that is pure love."

Through Kathleen telling her story, our lives are enriched, too. We see the love and humanity of life, death and family ties, and the potential to grasp our relations with our love ones beyond time and space and the transition of what is called, "death." This makes us more fully alive.

James Ainsworth
Denver, Colorado January 7, 2015

Introduction

This story is about my family and the tools I used to uncover my personal roadmap—dreams, books, psychics, workshops—all of which provided an uncanny and oftentimes hilarious ride through the metaphysical world.

It's a tale of an ordinary women's extraordinary journey through the maze of life, examining at a very young age the actions of her family members and how they handled many of life's most difficult challenges—including death.

Never one to be completely satisfied with being told how to think, I began searching for my own spiritual edge to hang on to when my religion left me unprepared to handle the deaths of my loved ones and the transitions that midlife brings.

More importantly, in the midst of my searching, I "accidentally" discovered Edgar Cayce and the A.R.E., which to this day I still use to expand my horizons. Because of Cayce, I have a renewed connection with God and found that life brought me back to my creator and myself, and the gifts I discovered are innately a part of one's being from inception.

This book is also about my own health issues and what it took to turn the tide to wellness and how I use that information everyday of my life for others, as well as myself.

In closing my story, while going through my parent's things, I am reminded of a particular "find" which reaffirmed my belief that my mother and I were definitely on the same wavelength, just in different time zones.

Dying is Weird

For Life and its expressions are one. Each soul or entity will and does return, or cycle, as does nature in its manifestations about man; thus leaving, making or presenting—as it were—those infallible, indelible truths that it-Life-is continuous. And though there may be a few short years in this or that experience, they are one; the soul, the inner self being purified, being lifted up, that it may be one with that first cause, that first purpose for its coming into existence.

Edgar Cayce Reading 938-1

In the parlor of the house was where grandpa lay in his coffin. That's what they did back then; they brought the dead bodies back to the home. Maybe the bodies never left. Maybe they just brought the coffins in. Either way, it was spooky. I don't know how long he was there. He could have been there one day or three, but I know it felt like forever to me. At age eleven, this was my first experience with death.

I remember grandma telling the family about the morning grandpa died. She explained that, the night prior, grandpa had slept downstairs in the parlor in a makeshift bedroom—he had been sleeping on a cot since he got home from the hospital. Grandpa wasn't able to climb the stairs to the bedroom anymore. He had very swollen ankles, due to what my mom said was congestive heart failure. In the early morning hours, grandma said she heard what she described as beautiful heavenly music. It reminded her of the little church choir in town but much deeper and richer in tone, something from out of this world. She got up and went down the stairs to check on grandpa. He was dead.

As I recall, there was an around-the-clock vigil over grandpa's body, with all the relatives and friends coming and going. It didn't seem like anyone was very sad; it almost seemed like a celebration of sorts, with lots of good food and lots of company. I wondered why everyone seemed happy. Why would someone have to be guarding grandpa at all times, working in shifts, saying prayers, and murmuring things about him?

When it came time for my mother to watch over grandpa, she insisted I join her. Reluctantly, I stayed by her side. My mom, recognizing the combination of fear and anxiety in my face, asked if I wanted to touch him. Oh my God, I thought, I can't believe that she is asking me to do this. Part of me wanted to and another part of me didn't. "Come on," she insisted. "Just touch his hand, it won't hurt you." I slowly walked up to grandpa and looked him over. He didn't look much different; to me he could have been sleeping. I wondered how anyone could know for sure if someone was dead if they didn't look any different.

Grandpa was a nice looking man with a nicely trimmed white mustache and a thick crop of white hair, sort of a Mark Twain look alike. As I looked at him, I wondered if his ankles were still swollen, but I couldn't see his ankles and I was not about to pull up his pant legs.

My mom said grandpa was eighty-three, and to me that was old. With a grimace on my face, I glanced in the direction of my mom. She was still looking at me, waiting. I put my hand up and with one finger quickly touched grandpa's hand.

I thought my mission had been accomplished, but mom was still looking at me expectedly. Her eyes implored me to try again. So I took a deep breath and I touched him once more. This time I could feel the lifeless cold of his flesh. It was horrible. That's it, no more of that. Mom smiled at me, and in her smile gave me the thumbs up for such a big accomplishment. I had to wonder, was this just some cruel trick she was playing on me or was she really this comfortable with death? After all, this was her father we were touching. I didn't remember touching him even when he was alive.

My grandparents were full-blooded Belgians. Their parents had emigrated from Belgium and settled in a Belgium Catholic community in Wisconsin. I don't recall receiving any hugs and certainly no kisses. I guess I felt they loved me, or at least they were fond of me, but I was never quite sure where I stood with them as a child. Obedience was the interaction in those days. Smile, shake your head in agreement, and go to church. If you followed those guidelines, you were loved, liked, tolerated, or whatever. That's how I felt. Many times grandpa and grandma would switch from speaking English to speaking their native language when they didn't want anyone to know what they were saying. For an eleven year old, how could you not think they were talking about you?

Grandma was a no-nonsense woman, very religious and proper. She had a ramrod straight posture and a high-pitched voice. She was the only grandma I had, and she always looked like a grandma to me, even in pictures of her when she was younger. The family was close and often got together, usually after church at a big Sunday dinner to play cards, or to gossip and laugh. The adults always ate first, with the men seated and the women waiting on them. After the adults were done, the children would eat. As kids, we never questioned our place in the hierarchy, that's just the way it was. Grandma could be very opinionated and was dead set against drinking, something my dad especially liked to do. In her opinion, his actions made him hellbound. Grandma told my mom that if it were up to her, she would burn down all the "taverens." That was how she pronounced taverns. Everyone mimicked her, chuckling as they said the word. She refused to ever set foot in one. However, she did admit to my mom that a glass of wine in the evening was very good for a person's health, and that she had some once in a while. Mom was sworn to secrecy.

Grandpa left his parents' home as a young man looking for work in the lumber camps. As a man of small stature, he found the lumber camps to be physically difficult, so he tried out for the camp "cookie" or apprentice, later becoming the resident cook. My mother said the reason he left home at a young age was because of his father, who grandpa described as harsh and severe, and a very strict Catholic deacon. My grandpa rarely talked of his young life, saying it was nobody's business. The fact that his father lost his parents and siblings to cholera in Belgium before immigrating to the United States may have had something to do with his harsh personality. After leaving home, my grandpa never went back.

It was at the lumberjack camps where grandpa and my dad met. Dad was also a cookie and then later a border at my grandparents' house.

Grandpa had this old shed in the back of the house where he had what he called a whetstone. The shed had a dirt floor and always smelled musty and wet. The shelves were crammed full of Grandpa's tools and lumber for his next undertaking. From picket fences to bird houses, something was always being built.

The whetstone was a big wheel that turned with a handle. Underneath the wheel was a shallow wooden trough where water sat to keep the stone wet. As the wheel turned, the bottom of the stone would be immersed in the water, which streamed off the stone as it went around and around. It was mesmerizing to watch. "This is how I keep my tools sharpened," he would say, and then ask me to turn the handle while he did the sharpening. It was a job I loved doing, just grandpa and me. It was certainly more fun than being with the women doing dishes and cleaning up.

Grandpa said he sharpened his knives to cut twigs from willow trees. He used the twigs to dowse for water, though he never talked much about how, exactly, he found it. Everyone said it was a gift he had. What kind of gift, I wondered? I watched him once; from outward appearances it seemed it was mainly a physical task. He would walk around an area, his eyes scanning back and forth with a willow twig balanced in his hands. All of a sudden the twig would quiver and start to bend toward the earth. Grandpa would stop and declare that that was where the digging should begin, and indeed, water was always found. I tried it, but dowsing never worked for me. I even held it over mud puddles to see if the twig would quiver and bend like grandpa said it would, but that didn't help either. It appeared what grandpa did was some kind of magic. Why did they call it "witching?"

From what I knew of my grandpa, he was a quiet, pensive, and religious man. But grandma heard the angels sing when he died—what did that mean? And then there was the story that was told by my mother. Grandma and grandpa were living out in the country when their first born child became very ill during the flu epidemic. Grandpa harnessed the horse to the cart and took off to fetch the closest doctor, who was in a town seven miles away. Grandpa had only traveled a short distance when he heard someone calling his name. He turned the horses around and, upon arriving home, found that his son had died.

I also had to wonder what part I played in grandpa's death. The day before he died, my nephew Jim and I were running around the house chasing one another to release our pent up energy, since it was too cold to be outside.

Jim was only two years old and was living with us after his early life seemed to be off to a rocky start when his mom and dad (my brother) divorced. My mother and father, both in their fifties, decided to raise Jim, much to everyone's surprise. I wish I knew how that conversation went when it was decided to bring Jim to live with us. How was that possible? My father did not have the patience or appear to enjoy children that much. But now I was enjoying being a big sister.

My mother hollered, "Stop running or you'll break my mirror!" Someone had temporarily put a large buffet mirror on the floor and she was worried we would knock it over. My mother was a very superstitious person. We had to knock on wood for luck, avoid walking under ladders, save the spiders otherwise it would rain, watch for black cats running in front of the car, and avoid eating bananas at night, as that would give you nightmares (or was that a health tip?) She had talked many times about the seven years of bad luck that awaited anyone that broke a mirror. Well, of course, one of us hit the mirror and it fell to the floor and shattered into thousands of pieces. Mom let out a whimper and covered her mouth. We were scared! Now what, I thought. Time stopped for a moment, and the echo of the glass breaking and my mom's gasp seemed to vibrate to the ends of the earth. This accompanied by the instant thought of seven years bad luck.

The next day came the news that my grandpa had died. If this was the start of seven years bad luck, we were in big trouble.

The Telephone Call

My second experience with death came five years later when I was sixteen. My parents received a telegram from my sister Beatrice who lived in Detroit. Her oldest son Mickey was missing and feared dead. It was a July 4th weekend and on a whim Mickey and his friend hitchhiked to Lake Huron where his friend's dad was vacationing. The boys never told anyone they were going. They borrowed a boat for the day and, when they didn't return that evening, a search party went looking for them. After searching the waters the boat was found drifting but the boys were not with the boat. A few days later the bodies surfaced. Funeral arrangements were made. My parents and I left for Detroit on the next available train. Mickey and I were the same age.

Living in rural Wisconsin was a lonely experience for me as a teenager. We had primitive living conditions—no indoor plumbing and no telephone. I loved spending summers in Detroit and staying with my sister. Even though we were 18 years apart in age and lacked the closeness that we would later develop, I longed for the companionship her children afforded me. I loved the green lawns of the city, the warm summer evenings, the bright city lights, and all the neighborhood kids that would get together and play ball. I made a lot of friends and Mickey and I had a special closeness. Every evening was filled with playful events. I was definitely a city girl at heart.

At this time in the early fifties, Bea was very active in the church. Being Irish Catholic, our family could be very passionate about what we did and her passion was evident in her devotion to the church. The hardest part about staying with Bea in the summer was the fact that I was expected to say the rosary every evening with the family and go to mass with her several times a week. In the evening, at rosary time, we would all gather together and get on our knees and recite out loud all the mysteries of the rosary—absolutely no reason would excuse us older kids from participating in this ritual. I didn't understand why we needed all of this religion; my summers were going by much too quickly to spend so much time on sore knees. However, I was expected to join in. No, not expected, *required.* So it was just a matter of getting through it and getting on to things I enjoyed.

Mickey, who was the oldest of six siblings, easily towered over the rest of us. Over six feet tall and lanky, he was a powerful presence. He had this mischievous smile that had us believing he always knew more then we did, but though his look was knowing, it was never divulging. He was an altar boy who took his duties very seriously. I don't remember hearing him complain about saying the rosary like the rest of us. He went to mass every day without complaint, but of course daily mass was required in Catholic school.

The church at that time seemed to be an extended part of the family, looking out for parishioners in times of need. They supplied clothing, food, and even money when needed, as well as being a source of personal comfort to many. It was that comfort that would help Bea through her tragedy, I think. Perhaps it was my age, but I didn't find the same solace in church that she did. I found myself wondering why she wasn't mad at God. After everything she did—the rosary, the prayers, and her devotion to the church—how could God let her son die? She sure got a raw deal and so did Mickey.

Due to the circumstance of his death, the casket was closed. A picture of Mickey was placed on top. I don't remember anything else except the picture. Was it an optical illusion? His deep black eyes seemed to have a depth about them that was surreal. I was looking at him and I felt he was looking right back at me.

Bea told my mother about the dreaded feeling she had the day Mickey died. She had this feeling of heaviness that she couldn't explain or shake. When the telephone rang, she was afraid to answer the call, as she knew ahead of time that it would be bad news.

The church was overflowing with people that hot July day, and their sobs resonated through the large building. Mickey's friend's funeral was held at the same time in another church not far away. My sister, who sat several rows from me, just stared ahead. She never cried and her gaze never wavered. She seemed to be somewhere else. For the life of me, I cannot remember seeing much reaction from my mother either. Immersed in my own grief, nothing profound was said to help me understand this loss. Not from my family, and not from the Priest. These women were nothing short of stoic. I vividly remember many times looking at my sister and wondering why she wasn't crying. It was very confusing to me and just a blur in time.

The large gathering at the church met up with the family and friends from the other church to form a long funeral procession through the city to the cemetery. The drive seemed to go on forever, car after car winding through long city blocks. Standing there at the cemetery, I hoped against hope that this was a nightmare that would soon end. But it didn't.

Later, friends brought food to a neighbor's house where all of us had gathered. There was a lot of small talk and shaking heads and trying to piece together the events that must have happened out on the water. The boys were good swimmers, someone would say, how could that happen? Maybe after boating they decided to go swimming and forgot to anchor the boat and it drifted away before they realized it. Or, someone else said, one of the boys could have gotten in trouble in the water and the other tried to help. I was watching everyone for some sign, some reaction, anything that made sense to me and then out of the blue someone asked us kids if we would like to get away and go to a movie. A few of the younger kids took the offer but we older kids just sat there hoping that someone would say something to ease this pain we felt.

Afterwards, no one talked to us about Mickey's death. We kids would gather in a secret location, away from the adults, and try to understand what had happened in our family. The whole ordeal was both sad and puzzling to us. The train ride back home to Wisconsin was a quiet one. No conversations about Mickey's death and no answers. Our Mickey was no more. ***Very Weird.***

Autopilot

It was these two deaths that prefaced this point in my life. I didn't have a clue about how death was preparing to alter my whole existence. The year was 1983, and I was about to lose two of the most influential people in my life—both in the same year.

For the first forty-five years of my life, I think I was on autopilot. I didn't think about it at the time, but looking back, I realize that life just happened. Before I knew it, I was married, had moved to Minnesota, and was a daughter, a sister, a wife, and a mother of three. I was a busy person, successful at my job, and managed a household. Because I was the youngest of my five siblings (10 years separated me from my next older brother) I became the primary caretaker to my elderly parents. They didn't live with us full-time yet, but they did spend the winters with us.

My brother Norbert was sixteen years my senior, and geographically and emotionally my closest sibling. We were best friends. Norb, as we called him, had the spirit of a teenager. He was always busy with something, usually entertaining everyone. He was the family planner. He wanted everyone to be together, whether it was to play cards, go bowling, or shoot some pool. He had a natural curiosity for life and could get anyone interested in the most mundane things. A born practical joker, his infectious laughter often had me laughing until I cried. There was never a dull moment with Norb around, and we loved being around him.

I remember the day when the cumulative effect of my brother's complaints about his sore right hip finally made me take notice. I suggested he see my orthopedic doctor. Prior to that, he had seen his company doctor and a general practitioner—both had prescribed muscle relaxers and rest. This went on for a year.

The orthopedic doctor examined Norb and right away, he knew that something was seriously wrong. The doctor then expressed with much urgency that Norb be admitted to the hospital. As it turned out, my beloved brother had prostate cancer. By that time, it had already spread to his hipbone and testes. Surgery and chemotherapy were the recommended course of action. Surely this would cure him, I thought.

Month after month, treatment after treatment, my brother expressed his concern. "I don't know why I am not getting better, I feel like my body is letting me down," he said hopelessly. However, despite his worry, the family tried to stay optimistic—after all, the doctor seemed confident in my brother's recovery.

The cancer ravaged Norb's body for four years, and all the while he struggled to accept the idea of dying. No one knew how to help him or what to say. What could you possibly say about death to someone facing it? Of course we had our catholic upbringing, but at this point in time I couldn't find any comfort in that. There had been many funerals in the past few years—aunts and uncles from both my mom and dad's side dying in their eighties. And there was grandma, who died in her sleep at the hospital at the age of ninety two. She was in for a routine checkup.

The church funerals did nothing to make me feel better about death. What did seem to help was visiting the cemetery every Sunday after church, talking about those who had died and visiting each grave. We all struggled with the same questions and still had no answers. I felt like I was revisiting the emotions left unexplored when I was sixteen.

Norb wondered who he could talk to that might provide some spiritual comfort. A local church sent a minister over, but the visit seemed too little too late. The family felt so helpless and ill-equipped to be of much spiritual help to him.

He and I did talk about love though. "You know," he would say, "no one in our family is very good at saying I love you. Mom loves us, I know, but for some reason she has never been able to tell us that, and dad doesn't say it either. I wish we could have expressed our feelings more in our family." He was right, of course. Our mother never told any of us that she loved us, and my dad was more of the silent type and talked only when he felt he had something worthwhile to say. Did that mean they didn't love us? No, but when faced with death maybe Norb felt he needed reassurance.

In March of 1983, my brother died. We were all devastated. At 61 years old, he left behind his wife and six children. My parents were grief-stricken. Norb was the one who visited them the most. He kept them laughing, tape recording their arguments, and instead of getting mad at each other they were able to find humor in their petty quarrels. To lose a child at any age is heartbreaking, and my parents were no strangers to that loss.

It happened the year I was born. Mom was forty-one and six months pregnant. She and dad already had five children at the time, the youngest being ten years old. My sister Loretta, who lived nearby, was the oldest. She was twenty-one, married, and had an eighteen month old son. He was my parents' first grandchild. Loretta had been fine the day before, washing clothes and standing barefoot in the dewy grass as she hung clothes out on the line. The next day, a very hot day in August, Loretta suddenly developed a fever. The fact that she was barefoot in the wet grass the day prior always bothered my mother; perhaps she felt that it was what made Loretta so ill.

Loretta's temperature rose quickly, with nothing seeming to help bring her fever down. The local doctor was sent for. He tried to help her as best as he could, but despite giving her aspirin to help reduce her fever, Loretta's condition worsened. She became delirious and within three days died at home. The doctor said it was spinal meningitis. The death was so sudden and difficult for everyone, especially my mother. Loretta and her were very close, a closeness that was made even deeper by the realization that each of them would have had a small child together.

Now who would care for her grandson? Loretta's devastated husband looked for help through his numbing grief. With a baby due in three months, numbering six in our family, my parents helped out as much as they could, but the tragedy was taking its toll. My father began drinking more and my mother took to her bed, deeply buried in her sadness. Family and neighbors were her source of comfort during her grief. Eventually, their grandson went to live nearby with his paternal grandparents.

My mother, who was now eighty-eight, was struggling with her own health. She had been to three different doctors in three different states, going through one test after another and no one could find out what was wrong. Mom had always been in good health, but now she was wasting away to nothing. Her appetite seemed good, but she had a cough that wouldn't go away. It was hard for her to do anything physical or even talk on the phone because of this continual cough. When I would call her she would say, "You do the talking and I'll just listen."

As my mother was prone to bronchitis, her primary physician ordered her to take antibiotics on a continual basis to see if that would help. "I don't like the way they make me feel," she would say, refusing to take them. I pleaded with her, explaining that the doctors thought it will help, but she cried out, "What the hell do they know? They haven't helped me yet."

My mother had always been a very attractive woman. According to many people, she looked like an older version of Jackie Onassis, with a great figure, even in her early eighties. Now this undiagnosed illness had all but erased the proud image she had of herself. I remember visiting her and watching her glance toward a mirror as she walked by it. With a thrust of her hand, as if straightening her hair would help, she would throw her hands up in disgust.

One day, while trying to encourage mom to fight for her strength and muster up a more positive attitude, I became exasperated with her. "Come on," I said, "walk with a little more vigor in your step! You're not trying hard enough to get well." With a look that could kill, she marched down the hallway with all the strength she could muster and responded, "What do you know about how I am feeling? I am sick, do you understand that?" I thought I did understand, but there was an underlying refusal to admit it to myself. The fact is, it was too painful.

After my brother Norb died, this strong selfless mother of mine became a changed person as her health deteriorated and her sadness deepened. In October we brought my parents to live with us, as living alone was no longer an option for them. Mom was extremely agitated most of the time and would lash out at anyone nearby. She demanded as much attention as she could get. At times, she would even throw her food or her glass up against the wall angrily. She begged me to quit work and stay home with her. "I'm not going to live that long, stay home and take care of me," she would say.

"You will be here for a long time yet," I argued, and I believed it. "Besides, I am only working part time," I would add, "And we have a home health care aide coming to help."

"It's not the same," she said. "I want you to be here all the time."

At night, as she tried to get some rest, she would often start coughing. My husband Ron and I took turns staying up with her late into the night. As she coughed, I would instinctively put one hand on her back and the other on her chest and say a prayer for each of us—one for her to feel better, and the other for me to get some rest. That seemed to calm her down. "Your hands feel wonderful," she would say. She would drift off to sleep and I would go back to bed. Just as I fell asleep, she would call me again to come and sit with her.

After weeks of this schedule I didn't know how I could go on. Each night I would pray for strength and the next morning I would seem to find the energy to go through another day. I had considered finding a nursing home for her, but I never mentioned it. "Don't ever think of putting me in a home," she said one day. "I would rather die first." It's like she had a premonition about what I could barely entertain in my thoughts.

Many times as I sat with her, my mind would drift back to earlier times. With the exception of my self-absorbed teenage years, we had always been close. She had this quiet strength about her. She was not an emotional person outwardly, so rarely did I ever see her cry. Life was very hard for her at times, but she seemed to have just what it took to endure the challenges. Along with her strength, she had kindness and compassion for everyone she met.

Just a few years earlier I had witnessed this quiet strength. Whenever I would call home to check and see how my parents were doing, my dad would tell me that my mother was resting. "What's wrong with her," I wanted to know, "is she sick?"

"I don't know," dad would say, "you can ask her." I talked to mom and she said she hadn't been feeling well, but that it was nothing to worry about.

After a few weeks, it appeared that her resting became fairly continuous, with her just getting up long enough to fix dad something to eat.

I told my dad we were coming to check on them, and after a six-hour trip to my parents' home, I walked inside and there was mom lying in bed. A terrible odor emanated from her bedroom. "Oh my gosh, Mom, what is that smell?" She tried to pass it off humorously at first, telling me that my nose was working overtime, but soon the conversation got much more serious. "I am dying of cancer," she said.

"How do you know that?" I asked in a panic. "And where do you have cancer?"

"In my female parts," she said simply. This was as close as we could get in describing her anatomy.

After much prodding and searching for clues, she told me her uterus had fallen and she was sure it was cancerous. She could hardly walk, she said, without it falling down, and then she would have to try and push it back in place.

We packed the two of them up and took them home. The next day off, we went to the doctor where he treated her for a severe infection. It seems that she had pushed her fallen uterus back so many times it became very infected, and with the infection came the strong odor which she thought was cancer. The doctor recommended surgery, but she refused and settled for a device that held her uterus in place. Needless to say, she mended well. Had she not gotten medical care when she did, she surely would have died.

Angels Among Us

My mother's courage and calm became apparent in other unexpected ways. Once, as a young teenager, I asked my dad to drop me off at a friend's house for a short visit while he and my mother went to town for groceries. He reluctantly agreed. It wasn't typically in my father's nature to go out of his way for something he considered unimportant, and me visiting a friend certainly wasn't one of his priorities.

My friend's house was a little off the main highway, over a railroad track and then along a frontage road. To get to the other side of the tracks, the road had a slight incline up to the tracks, which then leveled off until you were over the tracks. The road then declined on the other side.

Dad was driving a 1940 Chevy four door sedan. For some unknown reason, just as we got on the tracks, the engine died and the car stopped. With his foot on the clutch, he tried to start the car. At that moment, I looked up and saw the largest, most ominous looking train coming down the track at full throttle. The train's whistle seemed to blow frantically as we sat helplessly at a dead stop. With my adrenalin pumping like never before, I grabbed the handle of the back door and threw it open. "Jump!" I cried to my parents, as I placed my foot on the ground half way out of the door. I knew we needed to put distance between the car and us.

My mother seemed unusually calm. "Rock the car," she said.

"What?" I screamed.

"Rock the car," she repeated calmly, as if she were asking us to join her in a song. I slid back in and we all started rocking back and forth in unison. The car slid over the tracks, just as the train flew by. It felt as if all the blood drained from my body.

When I got to my friend's house, I was still frozen with fear, unable to speak or even cry. When I was finally able to tell my friend what happened, they thought that was the most amazing and frightening story they had ever heard. In the meantime, my folks continued on their way to shop for groceries.

Later, once we were together again, we discussed how lucky we were to survive such a harrowing experience. My mother laughed about how she was able to be so forceful in her directions to us. Me? I wondered how I ever listened to her.

Mom's presence of mind and her ability to react in record time made me wonder just what she was made of. While my parents visited us in Minnesota once, there was a situation that involved my neighbor's dog. The dog, which had always been tied up, broke loose of his chain, and as sometimes happens when dogs are continually chained up, he had become mad and aggressive, looking to vent his frustration on the closest human he could find.

My daughter and her friend happened to be those humans, and he took off running right toward them. They saw him coming and ran screaming onto our porch. They then grabbed the kitchen door and pulled it in front of them to protect themselves, leaving the kitchen wide open.

Hearing their screams, I went running toward the kitchen just as the dog charged across the room. Aiming right for my throat, he knocked me over backwards, all the while biting at my arms and hands as I tried to protect my face and neck.

My mother, hearing my screams, came running from the front room. Without saying a word, she picked up a chair and sent the dog flying across the floor. All the while, my dad was hollering from the front room, “For God’s sake, what’s all the commotion?”

“Thomas,” mom said exasperated, “if you would get off your *ars* (her choice of swear words) once in a while and check to see what the commotion is, maybe you could be of some help.”

As it was, the girls’ quick thinking and my mom’s fast reaction prevented what could have been a very tragic situation. A quick trip to the emergency room and a call to have the dog quarantined helped put that excitement to rest.

You Know, Dying is Weird

We were still grieving the death of my brother nine months earlier when my mother was admitted to the hospital with pneumonia. More tests were taken and more antibiotics were given, but she kept getting worse and the doctors were puzzled. An internist overheard the primary physician explaining his puzzlement over her inability to get well, and suggested a sputum culture be collected. One was taken and sent to the lab.

At one point the doctors told my mother she had emphysema, a diagnosis that at the time infuriated her. My mother never smoked, she lived in a rural area most of her life, and she was truly ahead of her time when it came to holistic health. She touted the ill effects of exposure to power line emissions, never cooked in aluminum pans, was an organic gardener, and believed in the use of herbs for maintaining health and healing. My mom was also one of the first people I noticed to always wash the tops on cans from the grocery store, claiming there was no way to tell where they had been or how contaminated they could be. She always had an idea on how to solve a health problem, from an apple a day to clean the colon to a garlic poultice for a cold—most of which I considered a bunch of hooey at the time.

One morning before going to work, I stopped at the hospital to see mom. She was unusually quiet and her gaze seemed to look right through me. There was something eerie about the way she looked at me, or perhaps she wasn't looking at me at all. I kept turning around to identify what she was staring at. What was she seeing? When I would talk to her, her attention would seem to snap back to me just long enough to answer basic questions. It wouldn't be long before she would be staring again with that far away gaze. However, there was one thing she said to me that day that I could never forget—*"You know, dying is weird," she said.*

When I asked her what she meant by that, she just looked at me as if she couldn't quite explain what she meant. What made that moment particularly unsettling for me was the fact that I still didn't believe she was dying.

I stayed with her for a while and then went to work. Two hours later, her nurse called. "I don't know how to say this," she said, "but I think you should come to the hospital as soon as possible. When I left your mom a few minutes ago, rather than asking me not to go as she usually did, she told me to close the door behind me. I think she may be ready to die."

How perceptive, I thought, of her nurse to recognize a change in her.

It was just a day or so before when the main nursing station told me how my mother kept using her call button, even though she didn't need anything. She seemed to just want someone with her at all times. They even had to disconnect it because of her unrelenting use of it. I talked to my mother about that and she said she did need the nurses, but they refused to come to her room. It was very upsetting to her. At the time, I took the side of the nurses, telling her how busy they were. Now I wonder if I should have been more sympathetic and tried to find out what she really needed. Maybe I could have helped bridge the neglect she was feeling.

On the way to the hospital, I wondered how it felt to be dying. I tried to put myself in her place, thinking of my own mortality while simultaneously thinking of my mom.

Does everyone go through this, I wondered, when they're confronted with a loved one slowly dying? Certainly I had plenty of time to think about things like this. Since she would never have wanted to go to a nursing home, this was probably a conscious effort on her part, if there was such a thing as willing yourself to die. She wouldn't have lasted in a home anyway, I reflected. Most women have the responsibility of taking care of others and are not very good at being cared for, unlike my father, who loved to be waited on. If left up to him, he would be hard-pressed to live alone and would likely need another woman to take care of him. I had ashamedly hoped that my mother would outlive my dad, as he could be very difficult to live with. He was a beer-drinker all of his life, and we tolerated that; however, if he managed to get some whiskey, his personality changed dramatically and he would be unbearable.

When I walked into my mother's room, she was taking her last breaths. Her breathing was labored and her eyes were closed. I tried to talk to her, but she didn't respond. I noticed the color and texture of her skin and it appeared to be transparent. The golden color of her wedding band stood out against the whiteness of her skin. She was lying on her side in a curled position, almost fetal-like under the bed sheet. Her hands were together. She looked very peaceful. Other than the sound of her breathing, I thought she was sleeping. Her breaths had an irregular cadence to them—sometimes slow and steady, other times there would be a lull in her breathing, with a quick deep breath immediately after as if to catch up. Then there was the rattle, a vibration deep within her throat. I had heard about that rattle and it worried me. Quietly and intently, I listened and watched. I called my family and waited by mom's bedside. I was void of emotion, not knowing what else to do or what else to say.

My mother died on that cold December morning with a

gentle sigh. If only I would have known what to say to her during this process, how to reassure her. But how could I? I couldn't reassure myself. Was this going to be part of my legacy, never having an understanding about how to comfort those who are dying? It wasn't that I was unemotional, it just seemed like I was at a loss as to how I could help.

Suddenly I felt the need to remove her ring. It was a simple gold band, but it was a symbol of a lifetime of happy times and sad times with my dad. I didn't want it lost like some of her other personal possessions, many of which disappeared while she was in the hospital, such as the wonderful cozy blanket that my daughter-in-law had made for her.

Getting the ring off her finger would occupy my mind momentarily, I felt. Any action was welcome, but the ring would not come off. Suddenly taking the ring off her finger took on a tone of desperation. As I struggled to remove it, panic set in. Can I get it off? I thought. What would people think if they saw me? My reasons for removing the ring now were getting beyond rational, it seemed. I debated between leaving it on her finger and worrying about it getting lost on the long trip to Wisconsin for her burial. As I continued to struggle taking off her ring, I remembered reading about how you could use thread to help you remove a ring, and I set my mind on finding a piece of useable thread.

Oh, for God's sake, Kathleen! Take a deep breath, I thought, and settle down. Suddenly, the ring slipped over mom's knuckle. I carefully put it on my finger. Hopefully no one was watching this scene, I thought. It would be embarrassing. I must be crazy.

Trying to put that little episode out of my mind, I caressed the ring on my finger. At least I have some part of her, I thought. She will need it back for the visitation, but for now it's safe with me.

I sat for a few moments, completely numb. I called the

desk to see if there was a hospital chaplain on duty. I hoped they wouldn't send the chaplain that I had often seen making rounds. He could never remember my mother's name, and often referred to a memo pad as if to reacquaint himself with her each visit. As far as I could tell, he never spent any time talking to her or comforting her, and that bothered me. I wondered why there wasn't a more personal approach to his cleric duties. Why would they have someone visiting the ill that couldn't even offer some comfort? His job, it appeared, was to give communion for the soul and to hell with the spirit.

Great relief came over me when I looked up and saw a different chaplain. He asked me if I was alone. I told him I had called my family and that they were on their way. He said he would stay with me as long as I needed him, and proceeded to give me a hug. The tears flowed easily. The words of comfort that came from him were a Godsend. I had never heard anyone so naturally gifted in knowing how to help ease my pain. He asked about my mom's family, and when I told him that my mother's husband was at my house, but I was afraid to have him see her like this, the chaplain insisted he should be with his wife. It won't be a reality, he said, if he doesn't see her.

Dad was brought to the hospital. When he saw mom, he let out a wail and cried. He reached over and patted her hands saying, "My Rosie," over and over. He couldn't believe his wife of sixty-nine years was gone. It was heartbreaking to watch my dad grieving. Trying to comfort him didn't seem to help him in his grief. It was a totally helpless feeling. I had never seen him like that before, and the ache in me was uncontainable. The chaplain said prayers as we all gathered around mom's bedside. The mood was heartrending and the room quiet and still. Suddenly, the coats that were on the chair fell to the floor with a thud, startling all of us. We glanced at one another amused. Did this have any significance to my mom leaving? Was it some kind of sign, I wondered? At the very least, the disturbance brought a little lightheartedness to the sadness we were experiencing. Two weeks after her death, the sputum culture came back. She died from tuberculosis, a treatable illness, had it been correctly diagnosed. For three years, it ravaged her lungs and her body.

The Police and the FBI

Dad wasn't doing well after mom's death. He was extremely depressed and unable to discern fact from fiction. He started wandering away from home while my husband and I were at work. Then he started accusing me of murdering my mother.

"I know what you did," he would say, looking at me with disdain in his eyes. "You poisoned momma!"

First I laughed, thinking he couldn't possibly be serious and waited for him to confess he was joking. Unfortunately, he was very serious. When I would try and reason with him, he would turn his head away and avoid looking at me. There seemed to be a shift in his thinking in the past few years, back and forth from reality to dementia, but more so now, this probably was accelerated by my mother's death. At 93 years of age, it was impossible to leave him alone even for short periods of time.

Finally I decided to look into a nursing home for him. It was a daunting task. Smells permeated my nostrils as I walked through the door of each home—the smell of staleness and sedentary living. The looks of despair on the faces of the residents made me sad. They would reach out for a touch as I passed by; they pleaded and begged to be taken home. Some residents rocked back and forth in chairs moaning like caged animals, confusion in their eyes. This was the last stop before death, I mused, how awful.

I don't believe I had ever visited anyone in a nursing home

before, and it was something I would never forget. Could I do this to my own father? It seemed to me to be a cruel existence. How could I possibly put him in one of these places? There didn't seem to be any way to compare the consistency of care from one home to the other. Who could you ask about care? If a resident had a complaint, would anyone believe them anyway? Here, I was in my forties, and I had just lost my brother and mother and now I had to put my dad in a nursing home. The burden had fallen on my shoulders and I was feeling resentful. My two remaining brothers had their own health and family issues that occupied their lives, and they lived hundreds of miles away. My widowed sister had just remarried, and although she was a source of emotional support, she also lived far away and was busy with her new life. Here I was, the youngest of the family, and it seemed I was the only person able to take charge. From the young age of eighteen, I was married and had three children in three and a half years. Now, when there should have been a break on the horizon, I was again a caregiver. No wonder I always needed to retreat somewhere alone. It was probably an automatic recovery system I had in place.

Eventually, I found a home that seemed to be somewhere in between, "I wouldn't put my worst enemy there" and "I guess this is better than wandering away from home and getting hit by a car." The first day I brought my dad to the home to live, it was a process for both of us. Dad was now going from a life living with his wife in a rural area on forty acres of land, being self-sufficient and independent, to our three bedroom rambler in a busy household of five, to a small room with a bed, dresser, locker, and easy chair if you could fit it. He could possibly have a television and some family pictures, if space permitted. This room was to be shared with another person and there was no say in picking your roommate. Window beds were acquired by seniority. No one went home from these places, so you know how seniority was achieved. I knew when I walked out that first afternoon, my dad would be under the complete control of absolute strangers. I printed my father's name in black permanent marker on each piece of his clothing—from his shirts and socks to his underwear. I had plenty of time to mull over my feelings during that time. Nothing of value was to be left for him, I was told. Now we were dealing with an unseen criminal element in a place where you have just entrusted the life of your loved one. And I wondered if he realized this was most likely his last address.

The second day at the home I greeted my dad with a hug and he just glanced sideways with that look again.

"The police were here today," he said.

"Why was that?" I asked.

"You know what they were here for," he said bitterly. "Because you poisoned momma, giving her those pills she didn't want."

He said it loud enough for others to hear. It was embarrassing, as well as so absurd. I let it go for the time being, chalking it up to his having a hard time adjusting to the move and wanting to justify why he was there by making me feel guilty. Maybe in a day or two he would forget this nonsense, I thought. After changing the subject to something more cheery, I tried to engage in a conversation with him, but he was still in his own world.

The third day I visited dad again. The daily visits were to ensure he was settling down okay and I was hoping he would find things to occupy his mind besides my alleged criminal action. Also, I hoped we could have a nice conversation. This day was no different than the last one. He wouldn't look directly at me and kept referring to the police and the FBI. The staff would quickly look in my direction and then glance away; I think they were wondering how I would handle the situation. I am sure they had heard it all at one time or another, but I had to wonder how they knew who to believe? It wasn't like they knew either one of us very well. One time, when my dad was still living with us and I was at work, he walked across the street to a church we occasionally attended and asked to talk to the priest. When the priest asked him how he could help, my dad told him his daughter had killed his wife. I had put her in the hospital after I poisoned her, he said, and that's where she died. Of course the priest came over and very tactfully asked a lot of questions about our home situation and expressed concern about my dad. When he left, I wasn't one hundred percent sure he believed me. In fact, it upset me so much I called a different parish and related the story to the priest there. He said he would come over and talk with my dad and see if he could help us out.

After his visit it seemed like the matter was cleared up. My dad was better and I thought the whole subject was laid to rest. Yet here we were again, dealing with the same upsetting accusations. Up till now, humoring him wasn't working, nor was ignoring the subject, so I decided I had one last option.

"Dad," I said, "if you ever tell me again that I poisoned my mother, I will not be back to visit you. You will be on your own. Do you understand that?"

He didn't answer me at first, so I asked him again if he understood what I was saying. Would he call my bluff, I thought? What would I do if he did call my bluff? I couldn't go on feeling apprehensive every time I visited him, but what about the guilt if I didn't visit? I reassured him that I would never harm my mother and he should know that. The crescendo of emotions I was feeling was unbelievable. It was difficult to keep them in check. After a few silent moments, he turned and smiled, appearing to finally get the message. We talked for a while about other things and when it was time to go I gave him a hug. He never mentioned anything ever again about me killing my mother. Somehow, he was shocked back to reality.

The staff, after I got to know them better, told me that they didn't think I looked like a person who could kill anyone. They thought it was rather humorous. Maybe they had witnessed situations like this before, but to me this was far from humorous. There wasn't any manual that I knew of that prepares a person for putting their parent in a nursing home. No Nursing Home Handbook for Dummies.

Out on a Limb

My dad had settled in at the nursing home and seemed content, yet I myself had suddenly felt immersed in deep grief. I missed my brother and my mother. My life had completely changed. No more Thanksgiving dinner's together catching up on family gossip. No sitting by the campfire with my brother and his wonderful baritone voice singing all our old favorite songs. For me, it seemed the intricate threading that winds from one person to another and holds us together throughout life was severed and couldn't be repaired again—not in this lifetime at least. The cords were cut. It was suffocating. I was so unprepared for death. But are any of us ever prepared?

It was all I could do to drag myself to work and get through the day. My husband and family tried to comfort me, as did my co-workers, but to no avail. I usually enjoyed my work but lately there didn't seem to be much I enjoyed at all. Up till now, there was no time for deep grieving. This succession of events took all of my energy, and now once there was time for reflection, I became grief-stricken.

It must have been my sorrowful disposition that prompted a friend of mine from work to bring me a book. She said the book covered many subjects, but the one interest I might have was how it related to death. Little gifts of kindness can help in ways we never know, I thought. This was very thoughtful of her. The book was Shirley MacLaines Out on a Limb. I brought it home and curled up in a corner of my bedroom, away from everyone, and started to read. It was hard to put it down. The story was great and yet the topics were so foreign to me. I read about meditation, dreams, reincarnation, Akashic Records, and karma, for starters.

Shirley wrote about psychics, one being Edgar Cayce who was called The Sleeping Prophet. This man fascinated me; I felt the need to find out more about him. This book was truly uncharted territory for me. I don't think I had ever thought about what a psychic was or meant until then. The closest I had ever come to learning about these subjects before was my mom's occasional reading of someone's palm to see how many times a person might marry or how long someone would live according to their lifeline. Of course, there was also my aunt who professed the ability to read tea leaves. However, neither of these situations produced any outstanding results. Although I do remember references to family members having prophetic dreams, which were actually taken very seriously and on occasion, there were those unexplained events that happened. Grandma hearing angels singing, voices in the wilderness, mom and the race with the train, and my sister's sense of impending doom as the phone rang.

Mom once told me about a time later in her life when her youngest sister Alice was a patient in the hospital. Soon to be discharged, my mother and her sister Eva decided to visit her anyway. Alice had emphysema from a life of heavy smoking and was routinely admitted to the hospital, until her condition improved and her lungs cleared, and then she would be released usually within a few days. While there, Alice informed them that she had visitors the night before. When my mom inquired who her visitors were, she replied, "Ma and Louise." (Louise was a sister who had died years earlier, as well as their mother.)

"You mean you dreamed they were here?" mom asked.

"No," " Alice said, "they were really here."

My mother said she never thought to ask any more questions, and always wished she had, because that night her sister died.

I read chapter after chapter of Shirley MacLaines' book, realizing that I would never stop with this one book. I would have to read many books on many different subjects written by many different authors to understand this whole supernatural concept. I was feeling some comfort as I started to believe that maybe life wasn't so random and chaotic as I had previously thought.

Once I was drawn in, a whole new world opened up to me. Classes, workshops, and more books that interested me were suddenly being dropped in my path. I wondered why this curiosity was never tweaked before now. This was a new adventure and I was going along for the ride.

The Journey

My family started to wonder what was going on. I was dedicating all my spare time to my search, leaving them to question my sanity. No one they knew had ever pursued anything like this before.

My husband Ron worried about what was happening to me. Usually a very quiet and patient man about my passions for different things, this one bothered him. He expressed his concern one day. Looking very sad he said, "I am worried about you and what you are doing, I feel our lives are becoming farther and farther apart." He recalled how I said to him, "Please don't interfere, this is something I really have to do for myself." There was a yearning, a longing, that I had felt for many years. I hadn't been able to share my feelings with anyone because I couldn't explain it. I felt constantly hungry, and yet my hunger was never satiated.

The difficulty for my family, I understood, was that I had always been there for them, at their beck and call, and now I wasn't. I was the one who kept the homestead humming with little grandkids running around and a guaranteed Sunday dinner. I was a convenient babysitter, watching sometimes six kids at a time. No one wanted to talk to me about my interests, I detected; it was only about their interests. How many times have I listened to a member of my family lament about something going on in their lives, and just when I needed the same consideration, they were ready to call in the men in the white jackets. Something wasn't right here. Don't mothers deserve the same respect? Aren't mothers entitled to their own life? It's my own fault, I surmised. My life has always been on the backburner. Now, with my children grown, married, and being parents of their own, I can have that freedom to search, can't I? But, I also wanted to share what I read and what I was learning at the workshops. This was good stuff. Once in awhile, because of my pleading, my daughter or one of my friends would humor me and join me at an event or seminar, usually hesitating until I offered to pay for them. For the most part, this was my solitary journey.

This whole search was a mixture of emotions. Sometimes I was anxious, sad, and overjoyed all at the same time. Other times, it would be humorous and downright bordering on bizarre.

One of my earliest workshops was on psychic intuition and energy work. I found most of the people in class knew a lot more than I did about this psychic stuff, and they were much younger than me too. Some had experienced finding things that they said appeared out of nowhere, like special rocks or coins—a sign indicating they were on the right path. Heaven-sent, so to speak. Some experienced astral projection, a concept they explained where you could leave your body behind and travel to different places, meeting people or seeing other parts of the world while keeping your mind intact. There were those that could see spirits and ghosts. I hated to admit that I couldn't relate to any of this. Many times, I wondered what I had gotten myself in to. Never had I seen anything out of the ordinary, or traveled out of my body. All this seemed a little far-fetched to me. I wondered if these people were on the up-and-up. Glancing around the room, looking everyone over, I often thought I must be the only sane one in the room. These were troubled people and I was glad I wasn't one of them. Of course I was never picked as one of the most aspiring psychic/healer in the class. Probably because I spent most of the time wearing a quizzical look on my face, asking myself what in God's name I was doing there.

The energy work was interesting though; the teacher would have us pair off and practice feeling the energy that emanates from each person. Using our hands as a guide, we would work within that energy field, holding our hands above the body and sensing any changes that might occur within the field. Somehow, I could relate to this. I could feel the energy and it was tangible. I remembered what my mother had said to me once about my hands feeling so wonderful. As I looked back, I wondered if she said that because I was touching her, or if there was something even deeper connecting us in those moments.

It wasn't long before I had enrolled in other workshops. What kept driving me to continue on this search was beyond me. I was being pulled, driven by a need. If I decided to slow down in my pursuits, I often found myself getting depressed. If I wanted to feel alive and whole, I needed to be studying and learning.

All this exploring was done with great enthusiasm and some naivety. Some of the teachers appeared to be very legitimate and some did not. At times, the situation would become laughable at the absurdity of it all.

One time, I talked my husband into joining me at a sweat lodge. He liked Native American culture, but he gently reminded me about some of our past adventures that didn't always go according to plan. I had a knack for side-stepping precarious situations while leaving him to meet it head on. Reluctantly, he agreed to go.

The woman that was setting up the sweat lodge assured me that it wouldn't be one of those real "hot" experiences. "If this is your first time," she said, "you will enjoy this one."

When we got there, we were surprised to learn that this was going to be a little different than originally planned. A bait and switch, Ron was sure of it.

Outside in the cold we stripped down to our bathing suits. Shivering, we got inside the warm tent. A medicine man was being honored with his first ceremonial drum. That meant that he would now be in charge of the sweat ceremony. Because of the sacredness of the night, it also meant there would be more hot grandfathers (rocks). The more grandfathers there were, the more steam that filled the lodge and the more the snow melted inside the tent. Ron looked at me apprehensively, "I don't think this is for us," he said. But I was encouraging and insisted we stay.

Suddenly, it started getting very hot and hard for me to breathe. The air was pungent and smothering. Without thinking of Ron, I bolted, leaving him trapped. I heard him say, "I'm going to leave too," but the medicine man said, "No, I think you should stay."

"You," he said calling after me, "sit outside as protection over the sweat lodge." A made-up assignment, I thought. I dressed and sat in a lawn chair like I was told. It was miserably cold and the wind was whipping around my body and filtering up through the webbing in the chair. Here is where I could use a lesson in astral travel, I thought. This is not much of a trade off. I wanted so badly to go to the car but I knew I would have been a dead woman.

Inside I could hear Ron's heavy breaths. With pleading in his voice, he mentioned how hot the air was getting. I thought about how his body had a hard time acclimating to extreme temperatures. This was not good. I was in big trouble. Everyone inside was giving him words of encouragement. Oh brother, I thought, he'll be eating that up. He stayed until the last grandfather's steam dissipated.

The one place I didn't want to be was in the car on the

ride home. The, "I don't know why I let you talk me in to these things," gets a little old. He should have felt great. Everyone cheered for him at the party afterwards, like he was some great hero. Me? I felt shunned. I am sure they felt I had tainted the ceremony.

The Ouija board was another pursuit of mine. Some of the articles I read about the Ouija board were disconcerting to say the least. Never having played with the board as a youngster, I had no idea what the hullabaloo was about, but I wanted to find out. If I asked anyone what they thought about the game, the answers varied from, "I wouldn't do it if I were you, it can be dangerous", to "it's only a game, what is there to worry about?" I decided the only way to find out would be to get one for myself and see what happened. Somewhere, I had read the instructions on the "correct" way of picking out the right board game. Tapping the resources of my mind where that type of trivia is stored, I retrieved the information and followed the instructions to the letter.

Go to the toy department, find where the games are displayed, pick out several Ouija boards and run your hands around and over the boxes, sensing the one that feels right to you. When you have narrowed it down to one, using that innate sixth sense, buy it. What other game has those kinds of instructions? And did I really want to be seen loitering around the game section flicking my hands over, under, and around these boards.

Reading instructions on the board at home, I became even more confused. This is a mystical game, it said, and should not be used frivolously. Ah, then maybe it is dangerous, I thought, though I figured most games are frivolous anyway.

The instructions continued, if you do use it in a frivolous spirit, asking ridiculous questions or laughing about it, you will get undeveloped influences around you. Well, the first person I thought about that struck me as serious and far from frivolous was my husband. He would make a good partner, I reflected. To my surprise, he jumped on board with me. Skeptical family and friends also joined us, and even though they had always cast suspicions on my sanity, they were now worried about my husband as well.

Give us questions about your deceased relatives, we would say, and we will get in touch with them. There was something disconcerting about playing a game that was suppose to conjure up spirits. It was like being a child and listening to a ghost story—everything becomes spooky and your imagination runs wild with nervous anticipation.

Family and friends pacified us and would agree, yes, that's what our relative would probably answer or that's what they would be doing. We wanted more proof and so we would log the questions and answers, but the answers were rarely consistent with the question. We both denied moving the oracle, which caused suspicious glances from one another and a few sassy comments.

One time when my daughter and I were using the board, something very different took place and we began receiving messages from someone who claimed to be from another time and place. Her story was very believable and we felt that, just maybe, we had connected with a real spirit. It was just a one-time occurrence, and it made an interesting story, but it definitely brought about more uncertainty as to whether the board really worked. Or maybe it did indeed work and it was the conductors that didn't work well?

One of the last times the board was used was when my daughter and friend were partnered. They both were quite skeptical and a little afraid at the same time, mostly pacifying me. When the question was asked, who gives us these answers? The message indicator skimmed across the board spelling out the letters D E V I. At that point, they screamed and threw the board across the room and would never touch it again.

That helped to put that adventure to rest. It was impossible to find anyone to play anymore. In the final analysis, I was still positively undecided as to what the Ouija can do, but it did make me feel like I was delving in to something I didn't understand. Maybe someday, after some psychic maturity, I will try it again, I noted.

Among the many supernatural subjects that interested me were haunted houses. If my memory served me correctly, I had neither been in one, seen a ghost, nor felt the presence of a spirit. I was ready though, and if there's one thing I've learned, it's that when you're ready, opportunities seem to present themselves.

One of the first times that I was aware of sensing something otherworldly was when my husband and I went to look at an old farmhouse that was for sale. It was a lovely fall day and the house was completely closed up, unless someone requested to look at it. We toured the downstairs first, noticing the dark furniture and dark paneled walls. Even the windows were covered in heavy dark drapery material. What kind of people could live in this dark and gloomy house, I wondered? The real estate agent didn't have any information on the owners—none that was worth sharing anyway. My husband and I then proceeded upstairs and started going from room to room. Suddenly, I felt I couldn't breathe, as though the air was knocked out of me. My emotions went from feeling very nervous and agitated to being extremely sad. The air felt dreadfully heavy. Looking around, we noticed the bedroom carpet had a large stain on it.

Us getting out of the house suddenly seemed to be a matter of urgency. We hastily made our way down the stairs with the real estate agent right behind us. As we were driving out of the driveway, we could see in the upstairs window what appeared to be someone looking at us. A later inquiry about the house turned up a little bit of history about what had happened. Someone had apparently died from a gunshot wound upstairs. *And*, we were told, the farmhouse was still for sale.

That first introduction into a haunted house wasn't what I had in mind. I was hoping for a gentle spirit who was just the run of the mill, average, happy-go-lucky spirit. I decided it was time to find a way to fine-tune my skills—to study, meditate, and work with someone who could teach me how to discern these experiences I was starting to have.

Coincidently, I heard about a weekly class on meditation and psychic development. The woman teaching the class was a very gentle soul and I liked her right away. She would be the first of many mentors I would have along the way. We worked on meditation, discernment, protection, and spiritual guidance. At times, there would be special guests to share their psychic gifts and talents.

One guest she had was a gentleman from the East Coast who was a palmist and gifted speaker. He was to talk about limitations and fears and stepping out of our boxes to experience more of life.

There were about eight of us seated in a large rectangular living room. One side of the room was covered in large windows. The speaker sat in an easy chair at the end of the room near the last window, and I sat kitty-corner across from him. He was a large man, clean-shaven, with a pale complexion. He explained to the group that he was still suffering from some physical problems relating to a bad car accident he had months earlier, and it was difficult at times for him to get comfortable.

The morning session went well. This man was very informative and interesting to listen to. He had a flare for speaking, was very animated, and his lesson felt well-prepared. When we gathered after lunch for the afternoon session, a strange feeling came over me. I sensed that something was going to happen that afternoon, and that I would not be able to control it, even if I wanted to. The closest I could come to describing the feeling was similar to the dictionary's description of an Aura—a luminous radiation; a subjective sensation experienced before an attack of some nervous disorders. Yet it wasn't a nervous disorder, it was happening.

Never before had I had that feeling, nor have I since. As this man spoke, I watched his flesh disappear from his face, and all that remained was a skeletal look. Surprised, and trying not to be obvious, I used my peripheral vision to try and observe the reactions of those around me. Could anyone else see what I was seeing? To my surprise, everyone just sat listening to his every word like nothing happened. This vision was disconcerting to me, and I felt like I was witnessing something from another dimension. I wondered if it was a premonition of things to come. The next thing that happened was this skeletal face started to change into many other faces, all superimposed over one another. The faces were similar to his, but not quite exact. Sometimes the face would have facial hair, other times not. One minute he had very long gray hair, and then the next he had shorter dark hair. As this sequence of faces took place, a silver energy, like liquid silver, encompassed this man and the two people who sat near him. Yet no one seemed to be aware of this silver light.

As the class ended, I felt mesmerized. It was difficult to come back, maybe not difficult as much as I didn't want to because whatever state I was in I was on a high.

After the session I told the speaker and class about the light I had seen. The speaker said he had asked his higher power to help him with his class because he had done no preparatory work. He thought that energy source was what I had seen. Because of his highly energetic nature, it appeared this liquid silver could have been his fuel, or energy source. The faces I couldn't tell him about. That all seemed way too bizarre to even try and describe. I considered that the faces represented his past lives as a teacher, all coming together as if past, present, and future were one, with no time limitations. This realization came to me long after the workshop was over, after I had taken time to reflect on what had happened.

Dreamland

One day a friend asked if I would be interested in taking a massage course. I eagerly accepted. After all, who wouldn't be interested in a massage? Unlike energy work, which was hard to explain and had the undertone of being labeled witchcraft, massage was simple and tangible.

For over twenty years, I was a part-time employee at a medical establishment. I was the scheduling coordinator for the inpatient staff employed at the hospital. It was something I thoroughly enjoyed. I'm not saying the staff thoroughly enjoyed their schedules, (that could be another story) but for me it was like working on a different difficult crossword puzzle day after day, and having the satisfaction of completing it. Fitting all the puzzle pieces together to staff a hospital (with the help of many others) was a rewarding experience.

Because of our close-knit office, I often had the opportunity to introduce massage to my co-workers. Everyone was ready, willing, and able to receive a treatment. There were more headaches, sore necks, and tense shoulders among them than I had ever seen in my entire life. People loved sneaking to my cubicle for a few minutes of stress-reducing massage each day, and loved being able to relieve their pain. Before long, the ladies in the front office could be seen working out the knotted muscles of each other so that they could continue to work the rest of the day with greater ease. It was catching on.

However, there was still something I wasn't sharing. Along

with massage, I was practicing my energy work, using my hands to facilitate the body's own healing ability. I wouldn't dream of telling anyone about my talent at the time, of course. The first time I brought up energy work, I was shot down quicker than a New York minute. This would have to stay undercover for a while. I would have to protect my newfound passion until the time was right.

No one seemed to remember how, in years past, therapeutic touch and massage were all part of the care given in hospitals. It was that added human concern and care that patients welcomed and which helped to foster faster recovery. Did they call it energy work then? No, then it was called love and concern for your patient. Everyone participated—the physicians, the staff, the cleaning service—and even the food that was prepared with extra care. How ironic, I thought, that here I was working in a hospital, so passionate about complementary therapies, and yet I still couldn't express many of my deepest thoughts.

Every book I read seemed to provide fodder for my inquisitive nature. I wanted desperately to share everything I'd discovered with my family and friends. Little by little, I would throw a tidbit out for my unsuspecting audience. It was especially hard at work. My five co-workers and I worked in a very close proximity to one another. We knew each other better than some of our own family members knew us. We shared happy times, sad times, and crabbed and laughed at one another. I knew that such a conservative bunch might not take metaphysical subject matter very well. These ladies were dyed in the wool, church going, no-nonsense individuals. What we had in common, though, was that we all loved a good debate.

I knew I felt safe discussing dreams with them. After all, everyone could relate to dreams, even though they had never thought about dreams relating to life itself. Dreams were always fascinating to me, though I had never researched or associated them with anything in my life. I had always had vivid, imaginative, and sometimes humorous dreams. One time, while relating a dream to my mother, she laughed and said, "Your dreams are so interesting. No one could ever make up that stuff."

After reading many dream books and taking some dream workshops, I began to journal my dreams. It was during this time that I realized just how important dreams would become to me.

Around the time my mother and brother died, some of my friends experienced their own losses. We started to talk about some dreams we were having about our loved ones. That seemed to open a door, especially as we helped one another analyze our dreams. The few book resources that I could refer to were shared with others. Lately though, my dreams were getting more interesting and opening doors to other realms. The one dream I would share helped me find some comfort with the deaths in my family, and I hoped an inspiration to others. It happened about six months after my mom had died.

It was during the day and I was sitting at my kitchen counter. Across from me at the kitchen table sat my mother and on the kitchen stool next to me was my brother. I remember looking from one to the other—my thought was they looked just like when they were alive. Not much different than our past visits.

"I can't believe you are here! You died!" I said excitedly to them.

"You really don't die, you know," my mom said.

"Can I touch you?" I asked.

"Sure," she responded, and so I reached over and touched her arm gently. It had always been her soft, fleshy underarm that I liked to touch and jiggle.

"You really are here," I told her.

She smiled. "Yes, and I am very happy," she said.

I looked at my brother, who had tears in his eyes. "I thought when you died you would always be happy," I said. My brother told me he missed everyone so much and that was why he was sad.

The next morning as I recorded my dream, I had mixed emotions. My mother sure seemed happy, but she was eighty-eight when she died. Could it be that if you died younger then there was more sadness for those you left behind, particularly if you didn't want to die, like my brother had expressed? I felt he had left this life kicking and screaming all the way.

His oldest daughter and I had talked frequently about her father's death and how she was adjusting. She told me how terribly sad she was, but how her dad's presence was the last thing she felt before falling asleep at night and the first thing upon awakening. It was very comforting to her. A few times, she thought she had lost that connection and started to panic, but her anxiety would immediately disappear when she sensed his presence.

Several months later, I had another significant dream. My daughter Lora and I were in a large auditorium filled with people, and from a long distance away I could see my brother walking toward me. He yelled out to us and called my daughter by a pet name he had given her.

"Hi pumpkin head!" he shouted.

"Look who's coming!" I said to my daughter, but she said she couldn't see anyone.

Norb was carrying an armload of books and looking very blissful. I pointed out how happy he looked, and he responded with a smile, "Yes, I am very happy, I am here for more orthodox education."

What did that mean? Was that because he was so un-conventional, I wondered? I asked him if he was okay, and asked if I should still say prayers for him. With a smile, he told me that I should say more prayers for him, and then he left.

This was so amazing, I thought. Here he was, a student again, and that would have been just like him. He was interested in anything and everything; and the prayers—I couldn't believe he was asking for more prayers. Maybe that was what the orthodox part meant.

I had to call his daughter and let her know that I had seen her dad in my dream and that he was looking great.

"That is so interesting," she said, "because the other day I woke up and didn't feel his presence anymore and I was okay with that."

It seemed to fit with what Cayce said about deceased loved ones staying around, helping us through the grieving process. Once we let go, it gives them the ability to move on and continue with their own growth.

Piquing people's interest with dreams was a good starting point. Bringing up past lives and re-incarnation was a lot tougher. That was a hard concept to sell. When you're raised with the belief that after you die there is a wonderful place waiting for us, (some of us) why would a person want to come back? No one in their right mind would leave paradise, would they?

In Shirley's book she talks about her spiritual transition in her forties, and here I was in my forties looking for a deeper meaning to life. I wondered if this was like a communicable disease that women caught in their forties, or a pre-menopausal problem. Attitudes were changing, especially in the women I had met at the workshops. It felt like I belonged to an underground community. I belonged to a sisterhood of sorts, and there were only certain people that I could trust with my covert activities.

During this psychic escape from reality, I had a dream. It began in a tent with a fortuneteller. She was dressed in gypsy clothes, with a crystal ball sitting in front of her. When I walked into the tent, she asked me how she could help me. I would like my fortune told, I explained. She said in a matter-of-fact tone, "You have all of the wisdom that you need within you. There is nothing more that I could add that you don't already know."

The next morning, as I was writing down my dream, I thought how I don't feel anything within me except confusion. But I knew that this was a special message for me. It seemed like the pendulum had swung from the far left to the far right, and I wondered how to achieve a balance in all of this.

A Lot of Bull

It had been five years since my mother's death and the fifth year on my continuing search. My dad was doing quite well at the nursing home. When we would bring him to our home for a visit, he would be anxious to get back to "his place" as he called it. All he needed was a beer once in a while—which was prescribed by his physician—and his can of Copenhagen snuff. I guess the doctor thought at his age, why deny him a few things that made him happy. A small chew of snuff, "Just the amount that would fit between the thumb and first finger is all I need," he would say.

Because he was only allowed to have snuff and a beer when someone sat with him, it was an infrequent occurrence. Whenever I would visit, he would right away ask for his snuff. He was like a child asking for candy and he knew what would happen when he took that first chew. It could put him in an altered state faster then a pot-smoking hippie. His eyes would get a little glazed over and he would take a deep breath and let out a sound of contentment. As he got older, it seemed the snuff took effect more quickly—it was his happy pill. He was one of those fortunate people that never needed any prescribed medication his entire life.

At times, he would be in a fantasy world, telling me about all the sexual parties that were going on in the basement of the nursing home. He could hear all the noises and he knew what was happening. Why, any man can have as much sex as they want, he said to me one day, shaking his head as if disgusted with the whole idea, but happy it was available if he wanted it. He would tell me who he thought was partaking in this sexual ritual, and then wait for my reaction. What do you say to someone who can't separate fact from fiction? I would just let him tell the stories and encourage him to stay away from such things. He would nod his head in agreement.

Unfortunately, dad soon suffered a series of setbacks. He fell in the shower after slipping out of the arms of a nursing assistant and had to have surgery for a broken hip. As that began to heal, he was given a styrofoam cup of very hot coffee that he set along side of his wheelchair pad. It spilled, giving him second-degree burns on his thigh. He also developed a large bedsore on the back of his foot that refused to heal.

During an appointment with one of his doctors, the doctor and nurse were helping him onto the table for an exam. Unable to move very well, he hit his sore heal on the wheelchair's footrest, smacked his bad hip on the edge of the table, and cried out in pain on the table as the doctor debrided his burn. I was near tears thinking of the pain he was enduring. Never one to dwell on sad things, he gave me a wink and said, "Don't worry, Kathleen. I'll get out of here alive yet."

At the nursing home dad was slowly recovering from his past injuries. Because of his attitude, the staff thoroughly enjoyed him. He wasn't one to complain, and his memory and Irish wit were still pretty sharp. Considering the injuries that he had been through, he was still relatively healthy. During his healing process, I started to use some of my innate healing wisdom that I was discovering I had. For a man in his nineties, my dad healed remarkably well. He had what was referred to as a strong constitution. Dad felt everyone at the home was old, and he often complained about being around old people all the time. Young people kept him feeling young, he said.

Dad was a good storyteller and people used to remark

about the funny things that happened in our family. He had a way of finding the humor in the ridiculous, and I believe that balanced out our lives. One story that sticks out in particular is the time that my sister tried to give him away to another woman.

It was my folks' sixtieth wedding anniversary and my dad took my sister Bea and me aside and said he would like to get my mother a diamond ring for their anniversary. Would we take him to a neighboring town about thirty miles away so he could pick one out for her? On a hot July day, my eighty-four year old dad—along with my sister Bea, my sister-in-law Alice, my niece Sue, and me—went shopping. Soon after getting to town, my dad determined it was too hot and we needed to go right to the tavern and have some beer (of course). After a few drinks, we took him to the jewelry store to pick out the diamond ring.

"How much do you want to spend," asked the jeweler.

"Nothing's too good for my Rose," dad said. "I want to spend a hundred dollars."

He pulled out a hundred dollar bill that he must have saved from his small social security pension and proudly placed it on the counter. In 1974, you could buy quite a bit more with a hundred dollar bill than you could today, but when it came to diamonds, not that much more. But dad had picked it out and he was proud of his selection, so he paid for it and off we went.

At his age, whenever my dad had a few drinks, the first thing to be affected were his legs—they just didn't want to work. It was as if his legs were made out of rubber and would flop every which way except the way he wanted them to go. So with that in mind, I said I would get the car and meet everyone on the next corner. The car was parked across the street and kitty-corner from where they were waiting. I intended to cross the street, drive to the next street, turn around, and pull up right next to them. While I was waiting for the light to turn green, I watched my sister pull my dad to a nearby car that was also waiting for the green light. She opened the back door and pushed my dad in. She then opened the front door and started to move a purse that was blocking her way so that she could get in. All the while, the rest of us were screaming and laughing, "Nooooo! Bea, you have the wrong car!"

Suddenly, she looked at the woman in the driver's seat and realized it wasn't me. She put the purse back, closed the front door, and yanked my dad out of the back seat of the car. With her head down in embarrassment, she dragged dad back to the street corner. All the while, the woman in the car was too stunned to say a word.

Once we got home, dad said playfully, "Rose, you'll never believe what happened to me today; they tried to give me away to another woman."

The recreational therapy director was especially good with the nursing home patients and the patients responded well. My dad loved music and had played the violin from the time he was a young man, so when he was asked to play at the Christmas concerts at the home he felt very important. He fell in love with the recreational therapy director. He was in his nineties and she in her thirties, but she went along with his fantasy.

"Get me a ring," he said to me one day. "I want to propose. She said she would accept if I gave her a ring."

"What kind do you want?" I asked.

"A ring from a bull's nose. I want it to be different."

My son Rick had just the kind of ring he needed. It was beautiful, brass, and came straight from a bull's nose. Dad proposed and the pseudo wedding was held. Everyone in the nursing home was invited. The bride wore faded blue jeans, a sweatshirt, and a doily from a nearby dresser for her veil. From the garden, she gathered a bouquet of flowers. She accepted the gift box he gave her, and when she pulled out the ring, laughter engulfed the home. Afterwards cake was served. This had been a special day for all.

The Scent of Death

It was in September of the following year when the nursing supervisor on duty at the nursing home called to say my dad had fallen again. He was on his way to the hospital in an ambulance to have x-rays to see if anything was broken. The fire alarm had gone off, she said, and one of the two nursing assistants that were with him went to check and see if there was anything wrong. When she didn't return, the other assistant left my dad alone on the toilet. He had gotten up by himself and fell trying to get out of the bathroom.

I was livid. I knew this would be the end for him. I raced to the home and walked up to the nursing station. Everyone's eyes avoided mine.

"Are you trying to kill him?" I shouted, "This is the end for him you know!" They nodded quietly. And it was the end—or at least the beginning of it.

Dad had suffered another broken hip. In October, he would celebrate his ninety-ninth birthday, but he was failing fast. He had an uncle that lived to ninety-eight and he always hoped he could live that long. His three sisters had all lived to be in their eighties. The longevity genes were strong in our family. I was glad he had lived so long because he had mellowed with age and became more family-orientated. Maybe he had worked out some karma in those last few years. He certainly had become more compassionate to my mom when she was so very ill, sitting up with her late into the evening and holding

her hand, trying to comfort her in the best way he co
When the movie On Golden Pond came out, everyone sa
that was my dad to a tee. He not only looked like Henry
Fonda, but he had the personality of the leading character
Henry played in the movie. The similarities were eerie.

Since I lived the closest and was always there for my parents, they called on me in times of trouble, like the time my dad called my work. At this time, dad was in his early nineties and mom in her mid eighties.

"You have a call from your dad," my co-worker Georgia said.

"Kathleen, you have to come and get me. Momma is kicking me out of the house."

Being 350 miles away, this would be no easy task, and it didn't sound like something my mother would do, especially at this age. I knew they argued a lot throughout their marriage, but I always thought it was more for special effects when any of us kids were around.

"What are you being kicked out for?" I asked.

"Well, the neighbor dropped off a little kitten and I wanted to keep it. Momma said she would have to do all the work to care for it and she isn't about to take care of any kitten and me too, so either the kitty goes or I go."

This would call for some mediation, I thought. If mom kicked him out, I knew exactly where he would want to live. The neighbor who dropped off the kitty was called and after listening to my pleading, they agreed to find the kitty a different home. Dad was safe, and I was off the hook—for now.

At the nursing home, my dad's life was slowly ebbing away. He would frequently call out, "Let's go, Let's go." When I would ask him where he wanted to go, he would look at me puzzled, like I should have known exactly where he wanted to go. When he was in the hospital for his broken hip, he his hospital room door and called my

"Come on in." Interestingly, there alive, but he always called my one ied.

eeks later, the nursing supervisor called and asked sion to withhold food from my dad. He didn't seem o be interested in eating anymore, and his condition was worsening. I told her I couldn't possibly give her an answer right away. Never before had I been placed in a situation like that. How could I possibly say he shouldn't be fed anymore? The more I thought about it, the sadder I became. That night, I decided to pray about it. The next morning, upon awakening, I reflected on the decision I had to make. In that moment, a feeling of calm overcame me and I felt very peaceful. It would be okay. It was his time to go. I called my family and explained how close to death he was and we were all in agreement it would be okay.

My sister Bea, who lived in New Mexico, came home for her last visit with our dad, as well as my nephew Jim, who lived in Texas. Jim, always one to talk and tease the nursing home patients, noticed one patient that would never talk or smile. Each day, she would inch her wheel chair ever so slowly around the nursing home, never acknowledging anyone, seemingly in another plane of existence. Each day, he would ask her how she was and tell her how nice her hair looked. On the last day of Jim's visit, when he realized he would not be seeing his grandfather again, emotion overcame him. He fell silent, not speaking to anyone. He took a seat in the lobby and put his head in his hands. Inching her way over to him, this wonderful lady took his hand from his face, kissed it, and put his hand back on his face. Then slowly, very slowly, she continued on her way.

Each day after work I visited my dad. He seemed to be

in and out of consciousness, but always sensing when I was there. I knew from some of the articles I had recently read that it was a good idea to talk to the dying, because even when they don't appear to be listening, they can hear and need to hear from you. My dad seemed to be struggling, holding on for some reason. Maybe it was because I told him I enjoyed talking to him about old times. My brother who lived close by was gone, so was my mother, so Dad and I did a lot of reminiscing. His short-term memory wasn't as sharp as it used to be, but he sure could remember stories from the past. He always provided a little Irish wit, with tall tales mixed in his stories.

It was time to let him go, I felt. He needed to hear it from me. I had decided that my next visit with him would be the time to tell him. I walked in his room the next day and he was in a deep sleep. I took his hand and told him I was there. His head moved back and forth, trying to get a fix on where I was at the bedside, and then he started to murmur something.

"Dad," I said, "it's ok to go and be with mom. You need to do that."

He smiled and said in a soft, loving voice, "Do you think so?"

"Yes, please go on," I said.

Silently, I asked what else I could do for him. The thought came to me to say a prayer. "Would you like me to say the Lord's Prayer," I asked. He smiled and said that would be nice.

The following day I was at work, sitting pensively by my computer, and thinking of my next task. All of a sudden an aroma filled the room. It was a different smell, hard to identify at first, but very familiar. As the scent filled my nostrils, I looked up and said, "Dad?" I immediately picked up the telephone and called the nursing home.

"How is my dad," I asked, feeling anxious. The nurse said he was still the same the last time they checked on him.

"Are you sure he is all right?" I choked. "Do you think he is dying?"

"No way to tell," she said. "He seems the same."

Okay, I will be there right after work as usual, I said.

I left the office a little early that day. Something was nagging at me to get on my way, but the harder I tried to leave work, the more I was delayed by one thing or another. I was thinking how I wished I had insisted they check on him right then, trusting my intuition. Finally, I was on my way, driving the ten miles to see him. I started to drive very fast. It felt so urgent, an urgency deep within my being. A city bus pulled out in front of me and I almost sideswiped it. Okay, I thought, that's it. Slow down and take it easy or you will never get there alive. I thought about the aroma during the drive. What did that mean? I had never experienced anything like that before. When I got to the home, I rushed to the door and was met by the nursing supervisor.

"We tried to call you," she said, "but you already left. Your father just died."

It was November first, All Saints Day, a Catholic Holiday. I considered that to be a bit ironic. Dad was anything but a saint, but he was catholic. *Dying is so Weird.*

Two weeks after dad's death, I was going through some of his belongings—a few small items and pictures that had meant a lot to him. I began reminiscing and touching each little article carefully. All of a sudden, I became aware of the same scent that had caught my attention a few weeks earlier at work.

"Oh my gosh, is that you Dad?" I said. The aroma lingered for a short time and then dissipated. My dad had made a visit, I was sure of it.

In the springtime of the following year, I visited my sister

Loretta's grave at a quaint little cemetery on the edge of town in the upper peninsula of Michigan—the place my sister had lived and died so long ago. Standing at the grave, I asked her if she had seen our dad yet. There it was again, that same scent that I associated with my dad, in the open air of the cemetery. Tears came to my eyes as I felt they indeed had connected. Maybe we all three had connected, but then again, maybe we had always been connected, more so than I could have ever imagined. It was a wonderful thought.

For me the death of my father was not a sad experience. It seemed like a pleasant journey for him. Was it because of the connection we had made? Maybe it helped that I was seeing death a little differently now. It all seemed to go according to some plan. I was at peace with that.

A dream I had after he died seemed to help with any residual grief I was experiencing. He came to me in my dream and asked me to go for a ride in a car with him. I was driving. As we drove along, he said, "I want to apologize for not being a good father, I feel very bad about that." He seemed quite sincere. Even though my childhood was not necessarily an easy one, it was something I never dwelled on for any length of time. But this visit I had from him in my dream solidified my feelings that everything was okay. I was relieved and happy for myself and for him.

The Connection

It appeared to me that the eighties era was a movement from one of acceptance to one of questioning. Life was not a neat package anymore, but then again, maybe it never was. The swing, I feel, had started a decade or so earlier, but the momentum was picking up speed and there were a lot of unanswered questions. My questions were common: what are we here for? What happens after death? How do we fit into the scheme of life? But most importantly, how do I find God?

Serious illnesses were on the rise. Misdiagnosis seemed to happen all too often, which meant that death was all around us. Physicians tried to treat the illness, but not the person, which made for unhappy and unresolved care in the medical field. Religious organizations didn't seem to be equipped to handle all the questions presented from a forum of sick hearts, scattered minds, and empty spiritual vessels. Everyone's misery was thrown in to a potpourri mix, it seemed, and we were all searching for basically the same answers, hoping to pull out of the mix just what we needed. The workshops I attended brought this out clearer than ever.

This journey had to be of self-involvement, self-development, and deeper insight into my life. I needed to go deep within and answer my own questions. Perhaps that was truly my journey. But how was that to be accomplished for me?

Through all of this, there was a fine thread of recognition

being woven through my mind from the first book I read about Edgar Cayce. This humble man was able to go into sleeplike trances and access information that went above and beyond the realm of knowledge known to most men. He was described as a medical intuitive with an extremely high accuracy rate. With only a persons' name and address given to Cayce in trance, he would give a diagnosis and cure. Upon awakening, he insisted on reading everything that was transcribed during his trance. He thought this might give him an idea of how his mind worked while asleep.

One of Cayce's trance readings that I refer to whenever doubts arise or sadness overcomes me is 5756-13. In a trance, Cayce was able to communicate with his wife's deceased family as though they were having a telephone conversation. Babies and young family members who had died years earlier were all together. Grandpa had built a house as a stopping point for those traveling to other planes of existence. He had been an architect while alive. Though not quite completing his earthly home, he was finishing up his work on the other side, putting out the welcome mat to all those who would be arriving at some point. When I let my imagination run wild, I can see it all. I hear the laughter, music, harmony, and squeals of delight anticipating someone's arrival—a big homecoming. It's all there, and for me, it turns sadness into gladness.

Since Cayce was a Christian, a Sunday school teacher, and an avid reader of the bible, the knowledge garnered from these trances (or readings, as they were later called), provided him with material that didn't quite fit into the religious paradigm. This was unsettling to him.

From a young age, Cayce appeared to be unusual. He had the ability to see fairies and little children that were around his age that he interacted with. They were spirit entities that others couldn't see. When his grandfather died in a tragic accident, he couldn't understand the sadness surrounding his grandfather's death, as he was able to see him often, many times in the barn working with the men harvesting tobacco.

His prayer was always to be of service to God and others. When in his childhood an angel appeared to him and said, "Your prayers have been answered," he felt he would finally be on the path to doing God's work, even though he wasn't sure what direction that would take him.

During this time I joined the A.R.E. (Association for Research and Enlightenment). Edgar Cayce founded this organization in 1931. Its purpose is to provide access to programs and materials that greatly benefit spiritual growth. It was at this time I also started a 'Search for God' study group. It was a wonderful opportunity to meet with other individuals that were interested in the same spiritual and metaphysical subjects that I was. My son Ron joined and had great insight into Cayce's work. Working with meditation, dreams, and the Cayce health remedies, I felt an excitement come back into my life.

One night, I had a dream in which Cayce and I were walking together on a beach. I could feel a deep sense of connectedness with him in my dreams. The conversation we had was brief; it was around the time The Search for God study group had ended. Mr. Cayce asked me if I had to leave. I remember telling him yes, but I would be back. The next morning, as I lay in bed, the memory of the dream and the energy became palpable. It really felt as though we had been together. Much later, as I looked backed on this dream, I remembered taking a hiatus from anything metaphysical and everything about Cayce for a period of time. I needed time to catch my breath I suppose, and I wondered if that was what the dream was all about.

But I did come back. Edgar Cayce's readings on health especially fascinated me. In the back of my mind, I wondered how my mother and brother could have been helped if I would have had this information on holistic health years earlier. My mother would have loved it. We really need to be our own doctors and try to be attuned to our bodies as much as possible. How else can we possibly stay healthy?

A Spirited Time

Being a member of the A.R.E led me to many workshops put on by members of the Association, including workshops on dream interpretation, psychic development, past lives, auras, and many others. However, the one that most interested me was on death and dying.

The Death and Dying Workshop was to be held in Virginia Beach, VA. As it seemed to be the case lately, I could not find anyone to join me, so I decided to take the trip alone. I felt an unusual contentment in my mind and body once I made up my mind to go. It was a deep, intuitive feeling that I had started tuning in to during moments when I doubted myself about something.

The flight out was uneventful, arriving to a cool and crisp November evening. I almost missed my connection in Charlotte, North Carolina, but as luck would have it I shared an airport shuttle with a very interesting lady, which made the ride to the hotel a pleasure.

The next day I walked the ten blocks to the A.R.E head-quarters just in time to join in the meditation and healing service. The energy in the room felt different from anything I had experienced before. Though it had a wonderful healing atmosphere, there was something else happening— it was as if the room was busy with sparks of prayerful waves. Energy was zipping back and forth, first to the heavens, as if to deliver prayers to be blessed, and coming back to the room and then off to the recipients.

The universal prayer lists included thousands of people, as well as the prayers that were said for our politicians, countries, and world leaders. We were encouraged to submit a name to the prayer list, which I did knowing ahead of time that I needed permission from the person being prayed for. The airways certainly seemed to be abuzz with prayerful intentions. Later I found out that the person whose name I submitted to the list greatly improved. We were then asked to sit in one of the many empty chairs for a personal blessing. Behind each chair was one of the members of the healing circle. The wonderful elderly lady who stood behind my chair and gave me a blessing whispered to me, "Never forget, the Lord walks with you and is always with you." With that, I gave her a hug and left. That experience stayed with me for a long time.

Having some time to kill, I decided to visit a local holistic store that carried many of the Cayce remedies that I used. The array of products and the hometown friendliness of the staff made this a nice stopping point. After I complained about the cost of taxi fare, a clerk asked if anyone was going in the direction of my hotel and if so, would they give me a ride. A young woman stepped forward holding a baby. Her appearance looked a little out of step with the nineties, more hippie-style. Not only was her appearance unusual, but she also had a strange way of speaking that was hard to understand. Thankfully, I understood enough to know that she would be happy to give me a ride. Before we took off in the car, she said a blessing of sorts about our safety and promptly ran over the curb. She got turned around and missed the road she wanted to take and made a turn right in front of a car. At that moment, I wondered what I had gotten myself into. That taxi fare didn't seem so high after all, I mused. The baby started to fuss and I asked if I could do something to help.

She told me that on her ride to the store she had to stop seven or eight times to try and keep the baby from crying. It was okay to pick her up and hold her, she said, so I did and the baby promptly fell asleep. She dropped me off at the hotel and I thanked God for my safe arrival and for her journey home. It was hard to tell if it was my euphoria from being at Virginia Beach, but somehow the feeling that I would get to the hotel safe and sound kept me from getting nervous about the driver. Maybe it was the prayer she uttered as we were about to leave that made me feel we had an umbrella of protection around us.

The next morning started with a spectacular sunrise. The shafts of the sun's rays rippled over the ocean all the way to the shore. It was a beautiful way to start the day. At the restaurant, I met two ladies that were attending the conference and they asked me to join them for breakfast. One lady was a hypnotherapist who said she was able to receive information on people through visions. She did a lot of work with a metaphysical institute out east and felt she had insight into who was on the up and up. I think she intended to check out the participants in the conference to see what her feeling was about them.

When I told her about my interest in metaphysical subjects, and especially death and dying, the first thing out of her mouth was, "Do you use the Ouija board? Because I will not have anything to do with anyone that uses a Ouija board, that can be the work of the devil," she said. Oh, here we go again, can she see it written on my forehead or what? Is this crazy kids' game going to haunt me forever? Of course, I denied ever using one and wondered if she really believed me. Quickly changing the subject and zeroing in on her psychic abilities that nailed me on the Ouija board, I thought I would ask her about my sister Loretta who had died the year I was born. I wondered if she could tell me if Loretta had reincarnated. Her feeling was that Loretta had moved to a much higher plane and so there is not that contact except once in a great while when she checks in to see how things are. It was a pretty generic overview. Many times I wondered if Loretta had reincarnated, after reading stories about family members reincarnating back in to the same families many years after their death. It was something I thought about often, looking for clues with each new baby born into the family. Did they have similar personalities, looks, talents, smiles etc.? I was like a detective, trying to figure out if this new child could be Loretta.

When I was in my teens I had a dream about Loretta. It was very clear and moving. The morning after my dream, I asked my mother if I had ever been in the house that my sister had lived in before she died. Since we had moved away from that town when I was very little, she didn't think I had.

"Well," I said, "if I describe the house, would you tell me if it's the right one? Because I had a dream last night and I was at her house."

My mom agreed, and so I proceeded, "In my dream, I was at the bottom of the stairs. The stairs were situated in the living room and at the top of the stairs dressed in a beautiful flowing blue gown was my sister. She looked down at me, smiling, and motioned for me to come up the stairs. At the top of the stairs she gestured with her hand, as if to show me around the room. It was one big room and it appeared to be a bedroom and nursery. She seemed very happy that she was able to show the room to me. Then the dream ended."

My mother told me that I had accurately described the house she lived in. If mom was surprised at the details in my dream, she never let on, but she listened with rapt attention. Since that time, I have never had another dream about Loretta.

Arriving at Virginia Beach a few days ahead of time, I was now ready for the conference. The selection of speakers for this conference was the best. Sometimes entertaining, at times very sad and serious, but they were always interesting. We had all lost loved ones and the hope that this conference would shed some light on how to deal with that loss was evident. That was what we all were looking for—hope. One speaker had the ability to communicate with loved ones that had died. He picked several people from the audience and amazed us all with his psychic gift of contacting the spirits. Another speaker had several near death experiences, and because of his experiences, he talked about being a changed person for the better on "re-entering" life. Death was no longer a worry for him. He had seen it all and it was good. One speaker talked about past lives and how they relate to our lives now. Rob Grant, another speaker from the A.R.E., took us through a meditation that seemed to call in everybody's loved ones that had passed on. The energy felt lighthearted and happy and that feeling spilled over into my room that evening and I bathed in its essence. How many spirits can you fit into a conference room, I thought? Would there be any limit? When the conference was over, there was a sense that the spirits all took leave around the same time. I wondered if they enjoyed it as much as I did? Cayce told about when he would teach Sunday School and the spirits would come and listen to his talks. He could actually see them in the back of the church; he said they were always interested in learning, the same as we are. Learning from mere mortals though? That was an interesting concept.

Because I was there alone, I used my free time for meditation and contemplation. I was really glad I had taken the trip by myself. It gave me time to journal and absorb what had gone on throughout the day. By the time I was ready to leave, I felt completely rejuvenated and ready to tackle the rest of my life. It seems that when I take in workshops and conferences of the spiritual nature I always have more vivid dreams and more acute, intuitive feelings.

One dream in particular occurred once I got back home from Virginia Beach. In my dream, I was lying in bed and someone was coaching me on how to have an out of body experience. As I lay there, still and alert, I felt my soul leave and soar through the top of the house and out into the skies, filled with the deepest of blue and twinkling stars. Because I knew this was my first experience, I didn't want to journey too far, so I remember telling myself not to overdue it this first trip and I turned around and started to come back. My soul was making a swishing sound as I traveled and I could see my body still sleeping in my bed. As I entered my body, I remember wishing I had visited someone while I was out and hoping I could have this experience again. Even though my experience was a dream, it did not feel like a dream. It was as though I was more alert than when I was awake, and on my return there was an audience waiting for me. When I told them of my journey, they all cheered for me.

The conference renewed my desire to study holistic healing, and this great interest and enthusiasm in wellness was giving me a new lease on life. If only I could have shared all of this knowledge with my mother, I thought. When she was interested in the benefits of healthy living, I was not, and now here I was, so passionate about what I was learning that I could hardly contain myself. With this courage and acceptance I decided to delve deeper into holistic health and energy work. I was finally coming out of the closet.

I became involved in hospice. After suffering through so many deaths in my family, I felt I would have something to offer those who lost loved ones or were going through the process of dying. Because I was interested in being a volunteer, I sat in on grief sessions to learn the best way to communicate with the bereaved and dying—most importantly, I learned how to become a good listener. During one of my required classes, my classmates and I were asked why we were interested in becoming a volunteer and whether or not we had lost someone close to us. As I listened to the stories being told around me and watched the anguish and tears, I silently prided myself on having worked through all my grief. My mother and brother had been dead for seven years, and I had cried all the tears and prayed all the prayers. All was well, I thought to myself. Yet, strangely enough, once I started telling my story, I realized that I wasn't as okay as I'd previously thought. Deep down in the crevices of my being, I still harbored guilt, regret, and plenty of pain. Undiagnosed illnesses combined with the inability to comfort my loved ones when they were dying brought unbelievable angst in me. It was a sobering experience. I then realized that no matter how long it had been since losing a loved one, we might never really heal completely.

However, I was shown I could grow through my grief. Working with hospice patients taught me more compassion, empathy, and understanding than I had known was possible, and it started another catharsis in my healing.

As I started to take a more proactive position in my life, the illnesses and mortality issues that I faced before began to seem more manageable. I began to understand myself—and how I viewed life and death—at a deeper level. The stories of near death experiences were riveting. Over and over again the stories would impress me with the same common theme, which to me indicated there had to be some truth in what all these people were experiencing. If that was the case, then there was hope that death was just another juncture in our travels. Reading the story about Edgar Cayce's life stirred my soul. His ability to communicate with his friends and relatives that had died, and seeing and playing with the little nature spirits, helped me broaden my views on keeping in touch with our loved ones after they have passed on. The idea that I wouldn't be sitting around doing nothing for all eternity after I died really resonated with me—that we carry over our interests and our desires and will even house with those that we knew and loved. To me, that makes death seem more like an adventure to look forward to than something to fear.

Also, Cayce said we were our own judge and jury. God is all-loving with each and every soul— after all, we were made in his likeness and that spark of God is in all of us. For God to banish our soul he would need to destroy a part of himself. After death, we view our life and all of our actions, good or bad. Whenever we have harmed someone, we feel his or her pain and that is our sentence. The more pain we inflict, the harder to absolve ourselves, but Cayce explains that no soul should perish unless it chooses to. How helpful this is if, in this lifetime, we feel we have gotten a bad rap. Somewhere, sometime, everything balances out. We shouldn't be too hard on ourselves for our failures because that is why we are here on this earth, to learn and grow. To me, that was a truly remarkable lesson to learn.

Visitation

At work, the closet door had opened and we started having thought-provoking conversations about religion, spirituality, health, dying, reincarnation, karma, and all other related subjects. Our discussions became so popular that others outside of our office would join us. A few of us even joined a daytime Bible class at work, but that didn't work as well. The Bible class participants were not very flexible in their thinking; they had their minds made up already on anything we sought to discuss, usually based on their literal interpretation of the Bible. Their strict points of view made me chuckle. Edgar Cayce said that if you are a Lutheran in this life, you will be in the next, and if you are a Catholic the same holds true. If you were not broadminded in this lifetime, you certainly won't be broadminded in the hereafter, unless of course a person worked to change his or her awareness. Our participation in that class only lasted long enough to get everyone riled up, it seemed. A Bible class that would have welcomed other viewpoints and encouraged discussion would have been ideal, but this was not the one.

One day an article in the local newspaper caught my eye, advertising classes that were being held at another local hospital. The classes were on holistic health. It seemed that there was some interest at this hospital about integrating traditional medicine with complementary therapies. The class was open to lay persons, as well as medical. This was a godsend,

I thought; here was my chance to study the very thing that had become near and dear to me: helping people to feel better the old fashioned way. After calling to enroll in the class, I was informed that the hospital had decided not to provide the classes at that time. It had something to do with the hospital hierarchy not being convinced that it was the time and the place for such a bold step. However, this helpful woman explained to me that there were classes being held at a college nearby that would likely suit my interests. This class was on Healing Touch.

When I took the first weekend intensive class, I knew I had found what I had been looking for. I loved the Healing Touch philosophy; they called it a sacred healing art. The goal is to restore wholeness through harmony and balance in the person being healed, as well as the healer. The quality and impact of the healing is influenced by the relationship between giver and receiver. Also, Healing Touch influences the energy system that is life. I knew I could do this, as I had already been healing people by touch before fully recognizing what that meant.

To take the classes, you did not need to be a part of any particular profession or specific spiritual orientation. There was a freedom about this philosophy; this class was open to anyone who desired to help another with sincere intent to heal. This energy work that had interested me for the last few years had now taken on a new meaning and I was finally able to legitimize it. It would take me two years of hard work to become certified, but I was looking forward to that.

Oftentimes I marveled at the direction life had taken me. I thought it was amazing how a single person's seemingly random, inconsequential interests and small pursuits, after a passage of time, could make way for life-changing opportunities. After all the courses and workshops I had taken, I was finally beginning to see the reason behind my interests. What keeps us going on a particular course, in a certain direction, with absolutely no roadmap on our journey? Sure, there are those that do have their lives figured out and seemingly know where they are headed, but what about those of us who go from pillar to post and somehow end up where we would like to be, had we really thought about it? **It** happens.

It wasn't hard to find people to practice Healing Touch on; some, however, just wanted good old-fashioned massage. They wanted something that they could feel and that gave them an overall sense of well-being, rather than something so esoteric that it could qualify as a crapshoot. My husband was one of those people. But after several sessions in Healing Touch, he agreed that it could be just as relaxing and stress-reducing as massage.

After introducing this energy work to my co-workers on a bigger scale, the interest grew and soon some of the nurses were enrolling in Healing Touch class and holistic therapies. The momentum was picking up for complimentary medicine. Our hospital even decided to open a medical surgical unit, which integrated Healing Touch work.

In the end, the program didn't last very long. For whatever reason, it was no longer a part of the medical unit. Some other hospitals took up the calling and, to this day, have a successful complementary treatment plan.

It had been a long road since the first time I became interested in energy work. It felt like I was trying to push through a road in an undiscovered part of the world. Trying to explain the unexplainable and yet coming up with results.

As I continued in my studies on Healing Touch, I started to question my decision. Sure, I had a passion for the healing arts, but by the time I would complete my training I would be in my late fifties. Almost everyone in class was at least ten years younger than me, more educated, and had many years ahead to pursue a career in this field if they chose to. Why did I always feel that I was the last to arrive for the party? Was I just a late bloomer?

Well, I did complete my training, and I felt the greatest sense of accomplishment I ever had. There was a dedication and commitment to becoming certified, and it was worth every moment. This training will always be near and dear to my heart and remains something I can use until my life's breath is no more. As you heal others you heal yourself, and I have found that to be incredibly true, not only in touch, but also in kind words.

For until ye are willing to lose thyself in service, ye may not indeed know that peace which He has promised to give—to all.

Edgar Cayce Reading 1599-1

An adjunct to Healing Touch for people was one for animals. It's interesting how that works, as animals have no preconceived notion on whether they will heal or not. If only we were so open and trusting. My training involved working with horses. It doesn't seem like there is much a person can do to influence a large animal's emotional and physical behavior, but given the right techniques, Healing Touch works wonders for de-stressing and relaxing large animals. Even the more nervous equine would be calmed down with energy medicine and a loving intent to enhance the healing process.

My first assignment was my oldest son Ron's, very anti-social cat, Midnight. One day my son heard some commotion down the street from his house and went to see what was going on. A car was stopped and the driver was very concerned because he thought he had hit an animal. Off in the ditch lay the cat. It appeared the cat was very badly injured, so the police were called to put him out of his misery. Just as the police arrived, the cat took off for home, arriving at the back door in tough shape.

"Could I bring the cat over," my son asked, "and see if you can help him?"

Midnight had a bleeding mouth, an injured nose, and other facial lacerations when he arrived to my house. It was late in the evening, so we decided to see if anything would help until the next morning when we could get him to the veterinarian. That evening, I did my Healing Touch trauma techniques off and on for hours and he settled in. The next morning he seemed much better, although his face was quite puffy. He healed very quickly considering the extent of his injuries and was back to his old sassy self in no time. Though Midnight didn't typically like anyone other than Ron, the two of us bonded a little in that experience.

My sister Bea, eighteen years older than I, never thought she was too old to learn. She loved to hear about everything I was involved with and was most encouraging. When I would visit her, she would invite the family over and ask me to treat them to an energy session. Arriving home after one of my visits, she telephoned to say, "You know, we all feel so much better after you leave." Hmmm…

Our times together were quite playful. She seemed to have a way of getting us into trouble, so our family worried about us when we were together. We actually became like children again. She had that influence on me.

One day she called to say she had some free time and wanted to know if I would set up a trip to South Dakota. One of her favorite spots was Crazy Horse Memorial Park. Next to Geronimo, Crazy Horse was her favorite American Indian.

"This is when I am coming," she said, "and I already have plane reservations."

"Okay," I replied, "I will get right on it and get back to you."

When I called for room reservations, everything west of the Missouri River had been taken. The reason, they explained, was because of the big bike rally in Sturgis South Dakota.

"Oh great," my sister said, "You and I and thousands of bikers—what could be more fun than that?"

My husband looked at us and rolled his eyes in disbelief at her words.

Thankfully, luck was with us and we were able to find rooms. My sister and I had a great time, just the two of us and thousands of bikers roaring down interstate ninety, and we both felt a wonderful, vibrant energy at Crazy Horse Monument. There was something indescribable about that place. It felt as strong and mystical as Crazy Horse himself.

My sister and I always had a strong, nonverbal connection with one another. Once, when her husband was very sick (a year after my mom died) I got the feeling that something wasn't right and so I called her up to see how everything was going. It was an early morning call, and Bea told me her husband wasn't doing any better.

"I am glad you called," she said, "are you thinking something might happen?"

"Well, I just had a strong urge to call and check," I told her.

Later that day, she called me back. Her husband had died.

She was my sounding board in my pursuit of spirituality. She had long ago traded the beliefs of her religious past in the hopes of expanding her wisdom. To say she was a believer in women's rights was putting it mildly. The fact that her own religion didn't recognize the role of women in the church bothered her tremendously. She would tell me how Jesus loved women, and how the church should in turn love women as much as he did. Women played an important role in the life of Jesus, she said, and she was always finding information to support her claims.

Bea was never quite sold on the reincarnation theory, but she loved the ideas put forth in all the books I read and passed on to her. We would talk endlessly on the telephone and on our twice a year visits with one another, never growing tired of our conversations on life and death. It seemed we could get a spiritual high from our discussions alone.

She would say often, "You know, God has a sense of humor."

I never asked her how she knew that, but she loved to laugh and always tried to find the humorous side to things. In one of my favorite readings of Cayce's he says,

"Cultivate the ability to see the ridiculous, and to retain the ability to laugh. For, know only in those that God hath favored is there the ability to laugh, even when clouds of doubt arise, or when every form of disturbance arises. For, remember, the master smiled and laughed oft, even on the way to Gethsemane."

Several years ago Bea confided to me that she was afraid to die. She didn't know why, but she said she had been worrying about it a lot lately. She was always quite healthy, so I didn't know why dying weighed so heavily on her mind. She didn't know either, but asked me if I would keep her in my prayers so she could overcome this fear.

One day she told me about a book she found called The Presence of God. She read it every day, she said, and it had become such a source of strength to her that it seemed her fear of dying was gone. She loved it so much that she went out and purchased one for me, in hopes that I could have a daily read that would inspire me the way it did her. It's a wonderful book, but I am not sure it resonated with me the same as it did with her.

It's the same with Healing Touch and any healing modalities or medicine. What works for one doesn't necessarily work for another. We need to find that which has the vibrations that attune our body, mind, and soul. As Cayce said, if you are of an aspirin mind, that is exactly what the body will need.

So in doing energy work, I found myself often disappointed when the person didn't respond in the way that I hoped they would, or if someone simply wasn't interested in finding out if they could be helped. What makes it all the more difficult is that we are living in a time where we need fast cures and fast recoveries. Fortunately, there has been a change in attitudes in the last several years, where patients are demanding more holistic care and are recognizing that it compliments traditional medical modalities.

For all healing, mental or material, is attuning each atom of the body, each reflex of the brain forces, to the awareness of the divine that lies within each atom, each cell of the body.

Edgar Cayce Reading 3384-2

One day, while struggling to try and put everything into proper perspective, I decided to go for a long walk. We had recently gotten a new puppy, who we named Ebby. She had escaped from the garage and I had to run all over the neighborhood looking for her, adding to my already fragile temperament. When I finally found her, I put her in her cage and took off for a brisk walk. It had been a habit of mine, when walking, to say prayers for all my family and friends that had died, as well as throw out some questions if I was concerned about anything. This time I decided to talk to my mother.

"Mom," I said, "could you give me some insight as to why I feel so low and feel so desperate to help people, especially those that don't want to be helped?"

But there was no answer—nothing intuitive, no special

feeling. My lamenting words took on a new tone. I went from asking sincere questions to being very skeptical about her ability to hear or comfort me.

"Okay," I said bitterly, "You are probably not here and maybe I am just fooling myself into believing that I can talk to you in the first place."

The sorrier I felt for myself, the faster I walked. All of a sudden I noticed a shiny object buried partially in the dirt. Picking it up, I cleaned the dirt from it and saw it was a dog tag. As I turned the tag around, the name on it came like a bolt out of the blue. The name was Rosie. That was my mother's name.

"Okay, mom," I said, "I've got the message."

Whenever I lose something, I call on my mother. Now, I don't know who from the great beyond is in charge of finding things. I know there is a saint that you can pray to, but I always liked to ask someone I know personally, especially if it is something a member of my family might remember seeing around when they were here on earth. Would they have a quicker sense of what I was looking for? Who knows, but the idea that they do brings me comfort.

It so happened that my mom had a little red address book. It was an old notepad measuring about three by five inches that she had gotten from a feed store many years before—probably a giveaway to advertise the store's products. Mom had pertinent information regarding everyone in the family in her little notepad—from births to anniversaries to deaths, it covered everyone. It was our family history and I used it often. I especially loved to look at her handwriting, which emanated familiar energy patterns. This little book was usually kept in a side pocket of my purse for quick reference.

One day I needed the birth date of someone in the family, so I went to check out mom's book. It wasn't where I usually kept it. I asked my husband to help me look for it, but it was nowhere to be found. We dumped everything out of my purse several times and it wasn't there. I thought of my sister Bea, who had visited recently, and called her to see if she took it by mistake—or maybe on purpose!

"No," she said, "I used it for some dates but I left it with you."

Could I have left it at my daughter's house when I was there a short time before? I asked, but she hadn't seen it. All over the house I searched for this little red book and again searched my purse. Finally, I asked my mom if she would help me find it, and then from there I tried to let it go. About two weeks later, as I was busily straightening out a drawer in my bedroom, I ran across some family rosaries. My mom had a beautiful rosary that I carried in my purse and I thought about putting it in the drawer for safe keeping. If I lost my purse, I thought, I would be very upset to lose this keepsake, so I got my purse and took the rosary out of the pocket I knew it was kept in. As I reached for the rosary, I discovered my little red address book right where it was supposed to be.

When I told this story to my sister-in-law, she laughed in that recognizable skeptical laugh that I had grown accustomed to hearing from so many people.

"You know, I have been missing a silverware set for years. It was a wedding present and I don't know where I put it," she said, tongue-in-cheek. She went on to tell me she had looked everywhere with no luck. "Maybe I will ask your mom to help me find it," she added playfully.

"Well, why don't you ask your mom?" I asked, "she probably could help you find it. I'm keeping my mom busy enough as it is."

So she asked her mom to help her find her silverware set. A few days later, her grandson was over. As teenage grandsons are likely to do, he was fiddling around in her kitchen, being annoying.

"Say grandma," he said, "do you know you have a back section to this drawer in your kitchen cupboards?"

He pulled the drawer out to reveal an interesting box—it was her silverware. I'm not sure she is convinced her mom helped her, but I love thinking that it can and does happen. All we need to do is ask.

I marvel at those that seem to never need reassurance concerning life after death. My uncle, when asked in his late eighties if he ever thought about death, responded, "Heck no! I'm too busy to think of stuff like that."

Maybe I am just a worrier. Even when I talk to people about my mystical/spiritual beliefs, I worry that I may be entering an area that is off limits. What if I am responsible for changing their minds and I am completely wrong in my thinking? How do any of us know what really happens to us after death? And yet here I am, enthusiastically telling people about all that I have read. It's hard not to share something that feels so right though.

One night, after pondering this question, I became quite emotional. Before going to sleep, I had a heart-to-heart talk with God about how I was feeling. I was so very confused and I needed to know if I was doing anything wrong, believing the way I did and encouraging debate and openness with others. The first night, I didn't remember dreaming about anything in particular. The next night I asked the same question. That night I had a dream, and in the dream a spiritual being came to me, infused in a wonderful light. It appeared like a male presence and the message was very precise and to the point. I immediately awoke from my dream feeling great about what I was told and the essence of the light was still with me. I repeated to myself what he had said and knew I would remember this profound message. I felt I didn't need to write it down. Well, I did remember most of the message, but I didn't remember all of it completely, which of course I scolded myself for later. The messenger said, "You, are not to worry, this is your path. Not everyone is on the same path, but this is the right path for you." It was an answer to my prayers.

Asking the powers that be helps broaden my view that all things are connected, and its okay to ask for anything. Divine guidance will monitor the difference between what you want and what you need. Maybe some days the spirits are more generous and it may be your lucky day to get a wish—a Heavenly lottery.

The Devil is in the Details

My very good friend JoAnn and I became fast friends when we took our Healing Touch course.

She is still doing her practitioner work many years after becoming certified. I, on the other hand, have branched out to many different interests, which have enabled me to feel as though I am continually learning. It's the endless searching and learning that keeps me passionate about life.

When she and I are together, we love to stay up 'til the late hours of the night talking about everything spiritual. It was on one of those late night tête-à-tête that we decided to take a trip to an A.R.E. conference. The conference was called the Sounds of Peace.

I told JoAnn I would make all the arrangements and she just needed to give me her personal information for the airlines. I said that I would call her after the flights were all scheduled. Everything went as planned, according to our time schedule. We were planning on a little extra time before and after the conference, as not to be rushed. After all, this was a peace conference, and should therefore be a relaxing, unhurried experience that allows us to be in harmony with the world.

The day of the trip arrived and the flight went well for a non-stop trip to the East Coast. We arrived at the airport, picked up our baggage, and headed to the shuttle area. Outside there were people milling around and I didn't see the shuttle we needed so I asked two well-dressed young gentlemen where the shuttle was to Virginia Beach. They gave me a puzzled look and then responded that they didn't know there was a shuttle to Virginia Beach. Now, I had been to a conference a few years earlier when I went by myself, and I knew there was a shuttle to Virginia Beach. They suggested I ask someone else that may know more about the shuttle service. Standing just inside the terminal in the midst of passengers coming and going, was a man holding a sign for a Mr. Edwards. I approached him and asked if he knew of any shuttle to the Virginia Beach area. He said, "You do know you are in New Jersey don't you?" That's when I realized I had booked the flight to Newark, New Jersey instead of Norfolk, Virginia.

This gentleman was very helpful and sympathetic. He told us of our options for getting to our destination. Our choices were Amtrak, Greyhound, another flight to Norfolk, or we could rent a car and drive the six plus hours to Virginia Beach. There was not one option that was going to be inexpensive or easy. Never having been in Newark or New Jersey for that matter, us two Midwest women had no idea what to do or how we were going to get out of the mess I had gotten us into. Finally, we decided to have lunch and contemplate our next move.

As we sat for lunch, I became very emotional thinking about my screw-up. "Now what are we going to do?" I said sorrowfully, looking at JoAnn with tears welling in my eyes. Like a good friend, she reassured me we were going to The Sounds of Peace Conference, Nurturing the Soul and the Earth. We determined that maybe we were being tested, and agreed to relax and trust that things would work out.

Since we had never driven to that part of the country before, we really didn't want to rent a car, but Amtrak was more expensive than we had hoped. The Greyhound bus wasn't leaving until almost midnight and getting another flight was very expensive. Plus, we still needed to get back to Newark after the conference. An airline agent said she thought we should look into renting a car. She suggested we go to Enterprise, as she felt they would be the most reasonable.

Off to Enterprise we went, and when we finally got there—via air-trains and shuttles—the staff all converged on us as though it was a very slow day and they were all excited to see us.

"Ok," I said, "we have had a very bad day. We flew to the wrong airport and we hear we are at least six hours away from Virginia Beach (we found that to be inaccurate), we need to be there by tomorrow morning and I have an awful headache."

One of the agents came out from the back room with some Excedrin and the other agents said they would do their best to make our day better.

The only vehicle they had for rent was a new eight passenger minivan with sixty-nine miles on it—nothing smaller, and nothing compact and easy on gas, just this humongous van for two small women. However, they decided they would rent it to us for the same price as a large sedan and it would only cost us $57.00 a day, plus tax. Of course, the gas tank had to be filled before we returned it or they would fill it for us at a higher price per gallon. So, with contract in hand and some very limited directions, we started out on the New Jersey Turnpike. Following the directions, and with very slow traffic around DC, we arrived in Virginia Beach eight hours later on a Thursday night.

The conference was wonderful and we certainly were filled with the aura of peace. I can't say enough about the feeling I get whenever I am there. The staff and presenters were top-notch and I always feel as though I am stepping back into a more peaceful time.

Because it took us eight hours to get to the Beach, we decided to leave Sunday after the conference. We wanted to get an early start and reserve a room at the Ramada near the airport, even though our flight didn't leave until 1 p.m. on Monday. We could rest and not have to rush, and maybe even get the car back a day early and save some money. Well, the winds were very high that day and we were discouraged from going the coastal way, which we were told would be quicker. Some planes were even delayed because of the winds. We decided to go back the way we came. Unfortunately, it appeared the directions we had on the way down didn't work in reverse. 295 to 95 to 64 was fine traveling there, but 95 to 295 didn't seem to apply on the way back and we got lost, very lost, for hours until we found ourselves back on the turnpike arriving at the Ramada eleven hours later.

The next day, after a leisurely breakfast, we were ready to take the car back to Enterprise, which was just a few minutes away. We decided not to fill the tank. We just wanted to be on our way to the airport. The same agents were there when we arrived, all wanting to know how everything went. We had told them where we were going and that we hoped to find PEACE in the midst of all that we had been through. They seemed very interested.

They began to check out the van, which now had over 1000 miles on it, and the gas gauge was down below half. The agent with the meter said, "Hmmmm, something is wrong here. I can't find this car in our computer system."

The staff all converged around the computer and looked and looked, asking for our names again and looking some more. I casually said, "Well, if its not in the system and we have had such a trying time in New Jersey—which by the way I am never coming back to—maybe this could be complimentary?"

Everyone kind of laughed as they continued to look for a record of our rental. Finally, the agent who was most interested in our story at the beginning, conferred a little with the others and then said, "Get on the shuttle, we are taking you to the airport,"

"But, you didn't give us a receipt of the charges," I countered.

They told us again to get on the shuttle and hurried us out the door to the shuttle. I blew them a kiss and away we went.

Now, what happened to the rental information, I do not know. Nothing was explained to us and we were too stunned to ask any more questions. It was divine intervention, I suppose, with the wonderful people at Enterprise playing an important role in helping our trip turn out to be one of our best.

Hot and Cold

It was a few winters ago that my husband and I decided to seek out some warm weather to ward off the chills of the cold Minnesota winter. We were Florida bound by way of Ohio, where friends lived. A part of the eagerness in planning the trip to Florida was in the hopes we could go to Hopkinsville, Kentucky and visit the graves of Edgar and Gertrude Cayce. Normally Hopkinsville would be near the route that we would take from Minnesota to Florida, but because we ended up traveling to Ohio we decided it would make more sense to stop in Hopkinsville on our way home from Florida.

Toward the end of our visit with friends in Ohio, I sensed an urgency to crisscross the states and visit Hopkinsville on the way down. My husband was in agreement and we started on our way.

I felt giddy with excitement. We arrived in Hopkinsville in the early evening and were greeted by very misty weather. The first thing we did was find lodging. Rather than settle in for the evening, we put our suitcases in our room and decided to go on a search for the graveyard. The receptionist at the desk said she really didn't know much about Cayce, but agreed that he was very important in those parts. She told us where we would find the museum and noted that the cemetery was on the edge of town. There, she said, we would find a big monument to Edgar Cayce.

"You won't miss it!" she assured us.

Hopkinsville is a nice city, with a population of around 30,000. Driving around, I tried to imagine what the city must have looked like in Cayce's day; the book store where he worked, traveling the streets to the Hill where Gertrude's family lived. If only I could have gotten just a glimpse, something to take me back in time. It didn't take us long to find the street where the museum was. Entering the museum, I was wide-eyed with interest amongst all the Civil War artifacts that were displayed. As fascinating as all that information was though, my main focus was on Edgar Cayce and the section dedicated to him. His desk, his furniture, his couch where he lay during his trance sessions that took him to other wordly realms and the wonderful photographs of his family which had a homey look and feel about them that captivated me. In a way, it almost felt like I was intruding in a very private residence. The area was roped off, but even if it wasn't I don't think I would have touched anything. Too many memories I felt were logged into all those personal items, the depth of which could never be erased. Like heirlooms that were passed down from generation to generation, picking up and storing the energy from everyone who touched them, mixing all the energy together and releasing the essence of it to each new owner. Edgar Cayce's personal items did that to me, releasing enough to satisfy me on an energetic level.

We lingered around the museum for quite a while, not quite wanting to leave such a special place, but also knowing it was getting late and we needed to find the cemetery. We had no trouble finding the cemetery; the gate was open and we drove in. No one was around—neither driving through the cemetery nor residing in the little house on the property. We started to drive down the roads looking for the memorial that we were told we couldn't miss, but we found nothing. Not knowing how to narrow our search, I asked Ron if he could just drive around and I would tell him whether he was getting hot or cold, just like the game we used to play as kids.

He started driving in one direction and I indicated he was getting cold. He turned around and headed down another road and that was cold also. After a couple of tries, he started in another direction that seemed to feel right.

"Keep driving," I said, "I think this is the right way, but go very slow."

As he drove, I opened my window and started reading the names on the graves. Some were sounding very familiar—the names of family members that I had read about. All of a sudden, there were some Cayce names.

"Stop!" I said excitedly, "this is it."

I jumped from the car and ran right over to Edgar and Gertrude's graves. As I stood next to them, the ground under me began to pulsate and the vibrations rippled through my whole body, causing such an emotional experience that I started to cry.

"Edgar," I said softly, "I finally found you."

Luckily, I was standing alone. I would have been embarrassed if anyone had heard me say that. It felt like he had taken my hand and led me there all the way from Ohio. By the time my husband parked the car and joined me, the feeling had dissipated. After spending several minutes inhaling the misty air and thanking my lucky stars for this experience, we left.

The next day, before leaving town, I wanted to see if I would experience the same sensation I did the day before, but it was not to be. We did find the memorial to Edgar Cayce. It was right at the front gate and we had missed it the first time around.

Watch Over My Ash

January 14th 2002,
I was lying in bed with my eyes closed and going through my list of daily prayers. Each year, the list gets longer, but it's a wonderful time for me to think godly thoughts and send blessings to all. A calm usually settles in when I start my prayers and I feel a spiritual connection. This morning was no different. Finally, I got to the last two names on my list—my sister and her husband. As I said Bea's name, a quick flash of light came at me. Thinking that was odd, I gave it but a moment of wondering and then got up. Ron was in the kitchen pouring up a cup of coffee and I mentioned to him what just happened and then promptly let it go.

About three hours later, the telephone rang. It was Bea's son calling. He had an abject tone to his voice that made me anxious. He told me Bea had died that morning.

"This was impossible," I said, "She wasn't sick."

She had plans. I just talked to her on New Years Day and she was vibrant and alive. She told me about her complete physical a few months earlier and she was given a clean bill of health. At eighty-one years old, my sister, who appeared so healthy, died of a massive heart attack. Her doctor specifically mentioned how strong her heart was and suggested she could live to a ripe old age like our dad had, yet in the end, it was her heart that killed her. She had complained in the last few days of not feeling well. In fact, she said her jaw hurt and had pressure pains in her chest.

"Do you want to go to the doctor?" her daughter asked.

"No," she said, "I think it's my tooth that's bothering me again and I'll just rest awhile and see how I feel."

She slept for twenty-four hours and then woke up feeling great.

That evening, she sat with her glass of Guinness and watched the rerun of the Mary Tyler Moore show, laughing through the whole episode. Her husband thought for sure she was just fine. He had wanted to watch the news about 9/11. There was always something on television about that, but Bea said they needed to watch more positive things.

"We need to laugh," she said, and laugh she did. In fact, her husband said he couldn't see how she could find the show so funny, and he went to bed.

The next morning he waited for her to come out of the bathroom so he could get ready for work, but she didn't come out. Finally, he knocked and there was no answer. When he opened the door, he found her lying on the bathroom floor. She had died early that morning.

Our last conversation was New Year's Eve. We talked about another trip to Ireland. In 2000, we had taken our first trip there with our nephew Jim. She was hoping we could do it one more time. There was one special place she loved. It was the Rock of Cashel, the site of an old castle. We had found very old gravestones with our family name. This was exciting to us, but it remained a mystery as to whether they were our ancestors. Still, that particular place had gotten in her blood.

She was also very excited about the parties they had been invited to. "This is going to be a New Year's to remember," she said, "and we are going to bring the New Year in right!" And party she did.

A week or two before Bea died, her husband recalled her

asking him to promise that if anything happened to her she wanted to be buried in Michigan near her first husband. It was something they had decided on years earlier—he would be buried next to his first wife, and Bea would be buried next to her first husband. But for some reason it seemed especially important that he remembered her wishes.

"Will you watch over my ash?" she had jokingly said to me not long before. She knew that the little cemetery in Michigan was just a stone's throw from where my daughter lived and she wanted me to keep watch over her. In hindsight, there were many clues that led me to believe she knew her time on earth was short. I wondered about the visit we had eight months earlier. Bea had taken Reiki training and was so proud of her accomplishment. She wanted me to see if I could feel any energy from her as she put her hands in strategic places on my body. Her hands vibrated a warmth and calm wherever she touched me.

"Would you check out my aura?" she asked. This was late morning and we were still sitting around in our pajamas, loving every moment we could spend together.

As I checked her aura, I could only pick up the color white. But it was a soft and radiant white.

A couple of months before she died, she told me about a dream she had. Years ago in Detroit, when she was involved in the church, she met a wonderful priest. When she went though the tragedy of losing her son, he was her spiritual saving grace. Through the years, he was a mentor to Bea and her first husband, always there to offer them spiritual guidance. Even as her views changed on the church's teachings, this quiet man remained a symbol of what was right about the Catholic religion. Although he lived in Ohio and she in New Mexico, they spoke often throughout the year, he letting her know about his family—deaths, births, and such—and she updating him about her family. He would always send his love to me through her. He knew about love I am sure. He offered the purest kind of love—spiritual love.

The year before she died, she was telling me she hadn't heard from her friend for a while and was a little concerned. Bea called his brother-in-law and was told that several months earlier there was a bad car accident and her priest friend was critically injured and lay in the hospital for a week before he died. She was devastated that she didn't know about the accident or how critically ill he was. She said she felt his loss immensely. Before she died, she said she had a dream where he came to her, looking so wonderful, and with a hug, his words to her were, "It's going to be alright."

She and her husband had been struggling with unresolved business issues and thought maybe the message pertained to that, but I think he came to her as a spiritual mentor preparing her for her transition. Certainly she felt a great relief after her dream. She could handle anything now.

Walking into a house where your loved one just died is extremely difficult. I could feel my sister's energy everywhere. In the evening, everyone had their own homes to go to or the out of towners stayed in motels, but I wanted to sleep in my sister's bed. The bedroom was across the hall from her husband. It was hard for me to distinguish between the grief I felt and the overwhelming presence that was there. As we gathered in the living room to discuss funeral arrangements, the tall halogen light in the corner would repeatedly go on and off. We would stop in mid-sentence and look at one another. *Weird.*

A few days after the funeral, in the early morning just as clear as a bell, someone called me. I got up and looked around, neither seeing nor hearing anything. I asked Bea's husband if he had called me that morning and he said no, he hadn't called me. No one else was in the house.

Why do they have the word "fun" in funeral? There is

nothing fun about it at all, unless of course you have an Irish wake. That's what the family decided to do. We were sure Bea would be joining us.

Because the family was divided by two religions, there were two services. The traditional service allowed us to put an empty glass of Guinness in the memorabilia but didn't allow us to express our thoughts and feelings about Bea. The second service didn't allow any Guinness glasses, but we were able to express how we felt, so we gleaned a little from both.

Next we needed to decide where to have the wake. What better place to have an Irish wake than in Old Town, New Mexico in a Spanish bar and restaurant surrounded by Saints sitting on little shelves on the wall? As we ordered appetizers and drinks, we also ordered Bea her Guinness, telling stories and singing Irish songs together. Laughing and crying seemed to be just what the doctor ordered. It was a lovely tribute to a lady who lived her life to the fullest.

Several years after Bea's death, I was in one of my relaxed meditative places. I started to relive the day I received the call. Everything came back to me in a heightened state. My initial denial, the shock, the grief, and regret—it all came tumbling back. As I continued to relax, the scene changed to what I perceived was a funeral home. Soft music was playing. It felt comforting and spiritual. As I was looking around in my minds eye, there was Bea's spirit floating upward. A star shone above as it pulled her spirit up. I felt I was there with her, and with deep emotion I asked her not to go, but she said she needed to. The scene started to fade and with a little deeper relaxation she appeared in ethereal form dancing and dancing. It made me smile to see her. I felt my left hand rise, reaching up to her, and when it felt as though we were connecting, all of my family started to surround me—not faces so much, but feelings. Even Ebby was in the middle of the group. Parents, grandparents, brothers, sisters, aunts, uncles, and cousins, all of this energy surrounded me. My brother Norb started to stutter, and I laughed and asked him why he was stuttering and he said to tease me and make me laugh. It was a speech disorder he had throughout his life. Bea and I connected with an imaginary ribbon and a heart to heart connection. She said I could tug on it if I needed her and she would do the same if she needed to get in touch with me. She promised to see me in my dreams.

Ebony Rose

We had pets all of our lives—when I was growing up and when we were raising our children. We had the usual cats and dogs, but we also had a pet raccoon, a skunk, and other creatures of nature. Some we didn't have very long, but having them was always entertaining.

By far, one of our most beloved and favorite pets was Ebony Rose. She was the one that had exasperated me in the early part of my story by running away from home, but she was also the catalyst for my connection with my mother through the dog tag.

Ebby was a gift from our daughter, who decided in our older years we needed a companion. She asked me not to tell her dad, as she wanted to surprise him. I mentioned to her that the few times I asked him if he wanted a dog he said no. He explained that it would be too hard to find a place for her when we travel. So I was surprised when I got a call saying she found a dog for her dad. Her cousin from Wisconsin knew of a litter of purebred black labs with papers, but there was only one left. At only $50.00, she was a female and the smallest of the litter.

"What do you think?" she asked.

In a strange, coincidental way, that very morning Ron told me about a dream he had where he said someone was trying to give him a little black lab puppy. He said the puppy really liked him. So, with that information, I said I think you should get the puppy for him.

Now the puppy was in Wisconsin, so her cousins agreed to bring her to Michigan. Our son Ron happened to be in Michigan a few weeks later and he brought the puppy to us.

Ron handed the puppy to his dad and his dad responded, "Whose dog is this?"

Once Ron explained that the puppy was his dad's, it was love at first sight. My husband and the dog were inseparable.

Ebby was a natural bird dog with no training except from her master. On one particular hunt with our son Rick and two other well-trained bird dogs, she outhunted and gathered more birds than the other two dogs combined. If they missed a bird, she would have that look of disgust. You could tell by her demeanor she was proud of herself.

One day while my husband Ron was fixing an overhead light fixture above the sink, I went downstairs to take a shower. He told me he had taken his hearing aids out so they wouldn't drop down the drain. Once in the shower, I pulled the shower door behind me and noticed I had pulled the door too hard and the door closed inside of the plastic lip, preventing me from opening it. I tried and tried and I couldn't open the door. I started to panic, knowing Ron had his hearing aids out and he would never hear me hollering from downstairs. He might find me dead in this shower in a week or so, I mused. I decided to start yelling for help and I could hear Ebby running up and down the stairs. I continued yelling and then I heard her nails clicking across the floor. Back and forth she ran. Faintly I heard Ron ask her what the matter was.

"Is mom in trouble?" he asked.

She shot down the stairs like a bolt of lightning and stood at the bathroom door looking anxious. Ron followed and opened the bathroom door and asked if I was alright.

"No," I said, "I am locked in the shower."

He had to get a screwdriver and take the door off so I could get out. Ebby danced and danced when she saw I was rescued. We were so proud of her, I felt like Timmy being rescued by Lassie.

She was also a part of Healing Touch. Ebby injured her paw on some barbed wire fencing that was located on our cabin property. Her paw was bleeding profusely and the gash was wide and deep. There were no vets around for 15 or 20 miles, and being a weekend, it appeared we would have to take her back to the city or try using a technique to cauterize the wound. I started infusing healing energy back and forth over the wound until the bleeding slowed. After a half hour or more, the bleeding stopped. We had her rest quietly for awhile and, after checking her wound, it appeared to have healed over and she was good to go. We did keep her activities to a minimum that day, and by the next day she was back to normal.

After eleven years of pure joy with her, Ebby's journey with us was ending. She had been diagnosed with cancer of the spine a few years earlier and now she was losing weight. Her hair looked like straw, having lost that brilliant black shine. Her eyes were downcast and there was no smile anymore. We decided we would ask her when she was ready to go. A few times we thought we had it figured out, just to take her to the vet and decide we weren't ready and bring her back home again.

One day, on a warm January weekend, we decided to take her to our cabin, her favorite place in the world. We had only traveled a few miles when she got very sick and vomited all over the car. It was time. I called the vet and he said we could bring her in right then. She passed very peacefully. We didn't do very well.

Her presence was felt around the house for many weeks after her transition. One night Ron got up and went to the kitchen for a glass of water. While standing at the sink, he felt Ebby by his side. He could sense her looking at him. He asked her what she wanted. He felt she needed permission to move on and that he would be okay when she left. He said, "Its okay Ebby, its okay."

That was the last time we felt her presence.

Have the lower forms of creation such as animals, souls or any life in the spirit plane?
All have the spirit force. The man, as made, carrying the soul force that made equal with the creator in the beginning, in that of relative production in its 'man's' plane of existence. Hence the necessity of development of that soul energy. Only when reached in that of the man, do we find the soul complete in the earth entities, or in man we find both the spirit entity and the physical entity.

Edgar Cayce Reading 900-24

A Vision and A Butterfly

A year after my sister died we were called to Detroit where my older brother Maurice lived. He had been ill for some time and lately had been getting worse. Our visit with him was one of revisiting the past and trying not to focus on the future, but he was very sick. A week after we returned home, he died. His wife said the day before he died he was cat-napping on the couch. As she walked by, he opened his eyes and said, "Did you see him?"

"See what," she asked.

"This beautiful man appeared to me and told me I was going to die, but I don't know what you will do without me," he said.

His wife said he had a peaceful look on his face and a glow about him. Prior to that, things had not always been that peaceful. He had suffered from dementia and was angry most of the time. This particular day though, he went through a transformation, and the next day was his transition. As my mother so aptly put it, ***dying is weird.***

Now here we are, September of 2011, and once again I am aware that my last sibling is very ill and I may have to make a trip to Detroit very soon. As I am considering what day we should travel to see him, I am outside moving plants out of the hot sun and watering them. As I finish watering the last plant on the deck, I stand up and a monarch butterfly hits me in the chest and sits there not wanting to move. I asked the butterfly what he was doing and why he landed on me (I felt it was a he). It just sat there not moving, clinging to my shirt. I gently slid my hand under its legs and it hobbled out of my hand onto the deck. I asked the butterfly if it was hurt and picked it up again.

"I will put you on my flowers and you can rest there," I said, but it fell on the deck again.

As I tried to pick it up once more, it went to the edge of the deck. I thought for sure it was going to fall the ten feet or so to the ground, and so I cried, "No don't go there, you will fall!" But all of a sudden it soared into the air and flew up over the trees.

It was so emotional for me for some reason. I told the butterfly goodbye and told it to be safe. This happened on a Tuesday. The day after, my brother was admitted to the hospital. By Friday, he was very ill and put in hospice. I called and was able to talk to him and tell him I was coming to Detroit and would leave the next morning. After a twelve-hour drive, we got to the hospital at eight o'clock that night. His daughter met us in the lobby and we went to his room. He was so happy to see us. We talked a little, but soon his meds kicked in and he was sleeping. I spent the night in the hospital and his daughter was able to go home and get some rest. I kept talking to him and telling him it was okay to go; we would be okay. I sang Irish songs, said the prayers that I knew were important to him, and stayed close by his side, talking to him about his journey and who he would meet when he left. It was a long list of those he would soon see. He had some very important religious people in his life that I felt were near and would be greeting him if they hadn't already. There was Father Solanus, a Jesuit priest who has been venerated by the Vatican (who Jim knew personally) and Father Middendorf, Bea's friend who was also a friend of the family, dating back to the time before Mickey died. There were also all of our relatives, too many to name but I certainly attempted it.

At one point, Jim let out a holler. I was standing next to him and asked him what was wrong.

"Help me," he cried, "I am falling! Oh no! Help me!"

"It's okay. I am here and I am holding on to you. You won't fall," I said trying to comfort him.

He had his hand around the side rail, gripping it tightly, and then after a few moments his hand relaxed and he was sleeping. The next day, he didn't communicate much at all and didn't seem to be very aware when we talked to him. Once in a while he would raise his eyebrows if I sang or prayed.

He died early Monday morning at 5:30. I was there with him. As I thought back to the butterfly, I felt it was symbolic of my brother's spirit. First the heart connection, and then the struggle to fly, and then the sudden change and his soul took flight.

My brother Jim was a WWII veteran and his coffin was draped with the American flag. After the church service, the honor guard played taps. I was honored and extremely emotional when his daughter asked the officer to present me with his flag.

The Cycle of Life

It was hard to think of selling my parents' house. After all, it was the place where I grew up, but that's what it had come to. Even though my teenage years were dotted with feelings of injustice, due to having to live way out in the country, my pre-teen years were quite the opposite. At a young age, my parents had bought a horse, which I loved to ride. Granted, it was an old plow horse we used to drag a plow and skid wood out in the winter, but it was mine to ride in the woods where I could let my imagination run wild. We also had dogs, cats, and other farm animals, and once in a while a pet deer. They all helped me wile away the time. Jim and I had a strong bond, even though he was nine years younger. He was always a source of fun and aggravation. Since he had lived with us from such an early age, it seemed more like a sister-brother relationship to me. My sister and brothers were much older than me and they had left home when I was young.

Because we lived so far away, it wasn't feasible to hold on to the property anymore. The house had been broken into a few times and some things that had meant a lot to me had been stolen. Oftentimes I wondered if I would be able to sell it, because for years when the thought would come up it would sadden me so much. I would have to quell my deep feelings by telling myself there was no urgency. I would try convincing myself we could keep it, but the idea wasn't feasible. It was very difficult to visit an empty house. Coming up the driveway, I expected to see my mother looking out of the kitchen window, with warm pies waiting for us on the kitchen counter. The house just held too many memories. It was better for me to stay away as much as possible.

Sometimes, when I tune into my higher wisdom, I feel differently about things. A calm comes over me and I get a sense of the right time and right thing to do. So it was with the old home.

There really wasn't much left at the old place. My daughter Lora and I had packed up things a few years earlier and I had taken them home to revisit at a later time. Handmade bedspreads, decorated pillows, costume jewelry—all were boxed to be gone through and given away. Mom had saved everything, from old photographs and letters to all types of cards. They were meticulously gone through as tears and laughter sounded through the old house. Every pocket on each piece of clothing had to be dug into, as she loved to stuff things in her pockets. From favorite agate stones to four leaf clovers in books, you never knew what you would find. It was a bittersweet task. We had packed her dress clothes, each bringing back that special occasion when it was worn. The twenty-fifth anniversary when she wore the blue-green blouse and tan skirt, the fiftieth was the golden yellow brocade dress. There was the sixtieth, a blue dress, and the sixty-fifth, a white jacket and slacks. For sixty-nine years, they had been married. But when she got so ill, possessions meant nothing to her anymore. By that time, it was a task just getting through from day to day.

My dad's leather strap was hanging precariously on a hook—the strap that he used for sharpening straight edge razors and threatening naughty grandchildren. It had that well-used look, with dark leather on the ends but soft and scuffed in the middle. On the medicine cabinet was an Old Spice mug, with a lather brush stuck in some hardened soap that had long since lost its aroma. Some books were still there, old classics and self-help books scattered around that smelled a little timeworn and musty.

My mother was always interested in keeping her self in tiptop shape, and my brother Norb shared this story on what was to be his last trip he took to see our parents. We decided to make it a family affair. My sister Bea flew in from New Mexico to join us and we headed for Wisconsin, stopping along the way for drinks and food. Norb, with his great sense of humor and ability to tell stories, told about the time when he and our brother Maurice were in grade school. One day Maurice arrived home from school earlier than usual. When he walked in the house, my mother was kneeling on the floor with her head in the oven. He watched for awhile and then called her name to get her attention. As she turned to look at him, he let out a scream. Her face was covered in a frightful green mask. It was the most horrendous sight he had ever seen. What was she trying to do, he thought, kill herself? She exclaimed that it was just some paste, which she put on to keep her skin looking young, and she was trying to harden the facial paste mixture by the heat of the oven. As we hooted and hollered about what she must have looked like, a gentleman at a nearby table walked over to us. You know, he said, I have never heard such laughter; you people sure know how to have fun. And our family did know about laughter, despite the ominous clouds in our forecast.

We finished looking through dresser drawers, making sure there was no money left stashed under the newspaper she used to line the drawers—money she squirreled away before my dad could gamble it all.

As we packed the rest of the books, one caught my eye that looked vaguely familiar. As I picked it up and read the title, I couldn't believe what I was seeing. The book was The Story of Edgar Cayce: There is a River by Thomas Sugrue.

The copyright was 1942, 1945. This was unbelievable that my mother had this book all that time. If only she had shared it with me, I thought, but when she was alive I wasn't even thinking about this extraordinary man. It was in her death that started me on my search. ***Yes, Mom, dying is weird.***

> *For many an individual entity those things that are of sorrow are the greatest help for unfoldment.*
>
> *Edgar Cayce reading 3209-2*